Postmodern
Public
Administration

Postmodern Public Administration

Revised Edition

HUGH T. MILLER

CHARLES J. FOX

M.E.Sharpe
Armonk, New York
London, England

Library of Congress Cataloging-in-Publication Data

Miller, Hugh T. (Hugh Theodore), 1953–
  Postmodern public administration / by Hugh T. Miller and Charles J. Fox. — Rev. ed.
    p. cm.
  Charles J.Fox's name appears first on the earlier edition.
  Includes bibliographical references and index.
  ISBN-13: 978-0-7656-1704-0 (cloth : alk. paper); ISBN-13: 978-0-7656-1705-7 (cloth : alk. paper)
  ISBN-10: 0-7656-1704-8 (cloth : alk. paper); ISBN-10: 0-7656-1705-6 (cloth : alk. paper)
  1. Public administration. 2. Postmodernism—Political aspects. 3. Policy sciences.
4. Constructivism (Philosophy) 5. Critical theory. 6. Discourse analysis.
I. Fox, Charles J. II. Title.

JF1411.F67 2007
351—dc22   2006012648

Contents

Preface

Postmodern

There has been a cultural blind spot about postmodernism. To the critics in the newspapers, it is as if postmodern thought is about to undermine everything fabulous about American life and introduce young minds to nihilism, black fingernail polish, and all-night linguistic turns. Postmodern thought is implicated in whatever has gone the wrong way in academia since mention was first made of it. "Over the last three decades of trendy poststructuralism and postmodernism, American humanities professors fell under the sway of a ruthless guild mentality," wrote one critic.[1] Postmodern thought is no longer a radically new category, but parochial malice lingers despite our wish that the enmity should have subsided by now. Perhaps there is, after all these years, still something important at stake that is threatened by postmodern thought.

Mainstream scholars need not be malicious to take exception to postmodern thought. The thesis of the present book indeed challenges mainstream presuppositions, and we should be able to take it as well as dish it out. Moreover, we could be mistaken in all or some of our interpretations; and even our most cogent propositions deserve the test of collegial criticism. Postmodern thought calls into question institutions as we know them, and also challenges ontological presuppositions about society and the individual. Postmodernism treats skeptically the notion that autonomous liberal-humanist citizens, can, through public deliberation, come to agreement about what is real, much less what is desirable, and then effectuate their desires through current representative/democratic institutions. Business-as-usual public administration may not want to hear about the decohering of governing institutions, but we hope this book contains food for thought for even the most ardent defenders of the status quo. Whether, in the media age, citizens are capable of conducting the informed policy discourse demanded by democratic theory is a pressing question.

Modernity was well described by those with sociological imagination, like Max Weber, who lived his intellectual life within its parameters. As an institutionalized cognition (an *episteme,* to use Foucault's [1970] conceptualization), modernity was buttressed by a dominant ethic of organizational rationality set to the tasks of caring for and controlling all aspects of nature and life. Ambitious and arrogant, the modern episteme was largely self-validating. As Lyotard (1984) put it: "I will use the term modern to designate any science that legitimates itself with reference to a metadiscourse . . . [that makes] explicit appeal to some grand narrative" (p. xxiii). In other words, modern systems assume for themselves potentially an all-encompassing God's-eye, or Archimedean standpoint, under which all can be rendered amenable to that system or metanarrative (Calinescu 1991; Rorty 1979). Another way of putting it is that there is in modern thought an indefatigable urge to universalistic monism, accompanied by an unrelenting instrumental rationality.

The modern metanarratives we will soon commence to deconstruct include the overhead accountability loop model of democracy, entailing orthodox public administration. Postmodernism is the refusal to describe humanity's progress as a rational process whose principles can be mastered, as though historical progress were one more step on the stairway to heaven or some other teleological end. Though immersed in the liberal traditions of modernity, postmodernism is nonetheless astonished by the Western faith in progress.

We want to resist the temptation to demarcate an epoch postmodern from an epoch named modernity, even though the term postmodern seems to make that claim. Richard Rorty (1991, 1) had this to say about the term *postmodern:*

> Heidegger and Derrida are often referred to as "postmodern" philosophers. I have sometimes used "postmodern" myself, in the rather narrow sense defined by Lyotard as "distrust of metanarratives." But I now wish that I had not. The term has been so over-used that it is causing more trouble than it is worth. I have given up on the attempt to find something common to Michael Graves's buildings, Pynchon's and Rushdie's novels, Ashberry's poems, various sorts of popular music, and the writings of Heidegger and Derrida.

This is actually a generalizable point: sex in biology means something different from sex in literature, for example. Instead of the term postmodernism, Rorty suggests, we should talk about post-Nietzschean philosophy, especially Nietzsche's legacy of perspectivism, "his refusal to admit the notion of a truth disconnected from interests and needs" (2). Rorty adds that "Nietzsche was as good an anti-Cartesian, antirepresentationalist, and antiessentialist as Dewey" (2). Where we differ from Rorty is that we are not as persnickety about linguistic specificity as he is. Instead of tossing out the term postmodern, we are willing to use it to refer to the ideas that Rorty referred to: perspectivism, antirepresentationalism, antiessentialism. The term postmodernism can point a reader in a particular direction, and with the help of additional words, sentences, and paragraphs, the author just may be able to communicate effectively with his or her audience.

Wishing for a common ethic or a unitary order is not a bad thing, necessarily, but it is not a postmodern style to propose that sort of program. The claims of such a system tend toward grandiosity and monism. Nietzsche (1974) urged us to begin by abandoning the most fundamental of totalizing ideas, the belief in God. "God is dead; but given the way of men, there may still be caves for thousands of years in which his shadow will be shown.—And we—we still have to vanquish his shadow, too" (Nietzsche 1974, 167). Lesser totalizing moves would be easy to refute after that. Nietzsche's perspectivism was expressed in his numerous other writings, especially *Beyond Good and Evil* (1885/1992) and *Genealogy of Morals* (1887/1992). Philosophical discourse shifted after Nietzsche and Darwin, away from universalism and toward contingency.

Postmodern thought is associated with some aspects of John Dewey's philosophy, much of Rorty's work, and, importantly, poststructuralist French philosophy (for our purposes, especially Jean Baudrillard, Jacques Derrida, Michel Foucault, and Jean-Francois Lyotard). Book-length contributions to postmodern thought in the public administration/policy literature include Stone (1988), Roe (1994), Fox and Miller (1995), Farmer (1995, 2005), McSwite (1997, 2002), Frissen (1999), White (1999), Spicer (2001), Miller (2002), Yanow (2002), and Catlaw (forthcoming), and in the organizational theory literature include Bergquist (1993) and Hatch (1997). In addition, Stivers's (1993) feminist critique of public administration stands as a powerful deconstruction of the (presumably neutral) masculine images of leadership, efficiency, and hierarchy that dominate the discourse. Intellectual trends in multiculturalism are also identifiable as postmodern thought. The common thread to these works is that they problematize presuppositions that were once taken to be foundational or immutable. Against essentialism, "So many things can be changed, being as fragile as they are, tied more to contingencies than to necessities, more to what is arbitrary than to what is rationally established, more to complex but transitory historical contingences than to inevitable anthropological constants" (Foucault 1994a, 458).

An unfortunate side effect of theorizing outside the banks of the mainstream is the need to employ different concepts using different terms. The language may be unfamiliar to readers intellectually situated in the public administration/policy literature. Many of the concepts we use are appropriated from other disciplines, and although we have aspired to concise, tight, and meticulous progression of exposition, reading this book may require reader effort. We want to thank you in advance for that effort; we hope it will be worth your while.

Acknowledgments

The first person to acknowledge here is the late Chuck Fox, who died in May 2004. He and I had contemplated a second edition of *Postmodern Public Administration* before his death, but he cannot be blamed for the revisions to the original text found herein. Some of the changes he might have agreed with; others maybe not. Either way, his impact on this book is ineffaceable and I want this revised edition to honor his memory. And so from here on, "I" will be "we," as it was in the original edition.

The work on the present version commenced after discussions with Harry Briggs and the M.E. Sharpe editorial board and after securing the copyright back from Sage, the publisher of the first edition. It was a gracious gesture on Sage's part to release the copyright, and much appreciated. Similarly, we appreciate Donna Fox's and Harold Fox's consent to having the book republished by M.E. Sharpe.

We would like to thank readers of various chapters who provided feedback and guidance: Thomas Catlaw, Gary Marshall, Göktug Morçöl, Michael Spicer, and Dragan Staniševski. We are also grateful to Mary Bailey, Gregg Cawley, Jennifer Eagen, Jack Meek, Ralph Hummel, and Lisa Zanetti, for helping to energize the book when it was envisioned as a different sort of project. Also, the ten-years-later symposium that appeared in *Administrative Theory & Praxis* in September 2005 helped keep the conversation about *Postmodern Public Administration* going. Richard Box edited the symposium; contributors included DeLysa Burnier, Cheryl Simrell King, O.C. McSwite, and Curtis Ventriss. All deserve our thanks. So, too, does Danielle Hollar Miller, whose kindness and generosity of spirit were much appreciated by Hugh in his time of messy office, sacrificed weekends, and restricted social engagements. Production editor Amy Odum copyedited the manuscript with laser-beam acuity. Harry Briggs of M.E. Sharpe should be recognized as a major force supporting scholarship in public administration/policy. He has steered the present project through its various obstacles and benchmarks, as he has done for many others.

Note

1. This quotation is from Camille Paglia, writing in the *New York Times* op-ed page Monday, March 6, 2006, A25.

Postmodern
Public
Administration

1

The Representative Democratic Accountability Feedback Loop

Orthodoxy

As an acceptable model of governance, orthodoxy is dead. Orthodoxy (Waldo 1948/2006) was that enduring prescription of neutral public administration ascribed in the literature to Wilson (separation of politics and administration), Taylor (scientific management), and Weber (hierarchical control). Orthodoxy, at its high point in the decades surrounding World War II, was a manifestation of the period that recent philosophers have identified as *high modernism.* We are referring to that point in time when the industrial economy matured and the ideology of technocracy and electoral-style procedural democracy prevailed in culture and politics, a period sometimes called "the American Century."

Since then, orthodoxy has died a thousand deaths, by a thousand cuts. The ever-apparent discretion exercised by administrators in policy formulation—not only implementation—makes a mockery of the Wilsonian dichotomy. Taylorism has been savaged by at least three generations of human relations social psychologists. The effort to sublimate political conflict into technical-rational domains was only sometimes successful. Strict chain-of-command hierarchy has been challenged by humanistic management practices, Japanese management theory, and participative decision making.

Despite its death and regardless of the eager academic pallbearers, the spirit of orthodoxy hovers over the study of public administration, insinuating itself in all theories of governance and in every actual public agency. Orthodoxy now has the status of legitimizing myth. It is the background assumption of all mainstream reform efforts. The contours of orthodoxy continue to shape the modules and sequencing of academic curricula. Reform efforts seek not to go beyond orthodoxy, but to resuscitate it by making it still more efficient, rational, scientific, and/or progressive.

Uniquely, the field of public administration is poised between, on one side, the theoretical endeavors of political science, philosophy, economics, organization theory, sociology, and social psychology, and, on the other, the daily practice of governance. Public administration scholarship is well positioned to bury orthodoxy and propose alternatives to it. Because academic public administrationists find themselves between practice and theory—we have been charged to educate the governors—we have direct knowledge of the maladies of orthodoxy.

The separation of politics from administration has been retheorized in countless essays since Waldo's *Administrative State,* but the representative democratic accountability feedback loop model blocks access to alternative democratic formulations of an administrative state. One of the paradoxical difficulties of the loop model of democracy is that the incessant demand for empirical verification and democratic accountability leads to the utter detachment of politics from democratic reality. As cynicism increases, managerial solutions deepen the problem. But first, what do we mean by the representative democratic accountability feedback loop?

The Loop Model of Democracy

It is widely assumed that in the United States *the people* are sovereign. Policy reflects their wishes. The majoritarian model of democracy is supposed to work like this:

1. The people are aware of what they want or need.
2. Competing candidates (or parties) for electoral office—political entrepreneurs—offer alternative packages of wants or needs that can be satisfied by particular methods.
3. People choose a representative by voting for which alternative package seems to best match their preferences.
4. Coalitions of winning entrepreneurs pass laws reflecting the people's choice.
5. A vigilant populace pays enough attention to the process and the results to judge the elected representatives as either successful or wanting.

6. If satisfied with the results, people will reward incumbents with their votes; if unsatisfied, they will vote for alternative entrepreneurs offering alternative packages.

Although less purely democratic than direct democracy, in which the people would both make and implement policy (government *of* the people and *by* the people), the above process is often judged to be the best we can get in a complex mass society (see Bachrach 1967). Although others act *for* the people, they are accountable *to* the people through the ballot box. The ballot symbolizes the political side of the politics-administration dichotomy. On the administration side are hierarchy and chain of command, enabling elected officials to both control nonelected career officials and superintend their carrying out of the people's will. Administrators must be neutral, malleable tools so that elected officials, who embody the will of the people, can have their way and be held accountable by the people for whatever does or does not get done.

Representation as Democracy

Among political systems, representation serves a parallel function in service to accountability: a promise of faithfulness to the democratic sovereign, *the people*. In this discourse, key terms supporting this promise of democratic faithfulness include *majority, vote, election, legislature*, and *constitution*. Policy reflects the wishes of the sovereign people.

The democratic overhead loop model presupposes the empirical presence of the people—but this is a highly problematic presupposition (Catlaw 2005). The phrase *the people* masks the radical absence of any such monistic aggregation, of any such consensus. Instead, there are multiple perspectives, multiple interests, and vast fields of conflict (Miller 2002).

Different types and intensities of conflict are expressed on multiple playing fields of public policy. Some conflict occurs against a background of subgroup consensus in a narrowly constituted policy community, and may be low intensity. At the other extreme, we might find broad-based ideological conflict over the role of government. Lowi's (1964) classic article on policy arenas made this point aptly, and amendments to it have sharpened the analysis. Players in the policy process petition government not only about grievances, but also for largesse. Terms such as *military-industrial complex, iron triangles, pork-barrel politics*, and *policy community* capture the closed nature of everyday policymaking, directing the eye toward the particularistic and narrow perspectives that cannot credibly be said to be fundamentally concerned with the public interest.

Analyses in public administration/policy typically take for granted the legitimacy and functional success of the loop model, and further assume that elected officials represent the people in a nonproblematic way. But the robustness of venerable values such as *the public interest, the common good*, or *the people's will*, as manifest in actions by the sovereign (represented by elected officials) now seems flabby and spongy. The loop is yielding some ground after years of criticism. It is too-readily apparent that particularistic policy actors dominate everyday, outside-the-limelight policymaking, and their interests only coincidentally embody less particular interests that would gesture more vigorously toward the common good (McConnell 1966).

The common good is not thereby rendered a futile concept. To the contrary, it is especially useful in conceptualizing "tragedy-of-the-commons"-type problems (Hardin 1968) in which community-regarding actions are undermined by self-regarding actions; useful, too, in public policy considerations such as common defense, old age insurance, health insurance, or unemployment insurance. On the other hand, many policy institutions allude to the name of the public interest while advancing particularistic interests. Defense contractors are notorious for this, but it is also notable that the food stamp program gets its political wherewithal not from poor people, but from agribusiness and grocers. The Food and Nutrition Service, which administers the program, is located in the U.S. Department of Agriculture.

Critiques of these aspects of particularistic, insider government have been standard for quite some time (see Fritschler 1975). The criticism we are offering is directed at systemic presuppositions. The complex web of relationships invoked by the network metaphor, privatization, interagency task forces, representative bureaucracy, or open-system organizations creates large problems for the sovereignty of the people. With knowledge as their key resource, public administrators and policy implementers lead others to value their expertise and understanding of important dimensions of the problem. Knowledgeable people, along with others in need of answers, join efforts and work together. In the process of interaction and reciprocal influence, the issues become clarified, relevant evidence is shared and debated, and alternative solutions are proposed.

These trends are not always favorably acknowledged. Lowi (1969) calls for a return to a formal, representative democracy, expressing a desire to reestablish the rights of the legislature. But the ever-increasing evidence of extraformal political dynamics reflects a desire for say-so in public policy debates, formalities notwithstanding. It would be hard to claim, any more, that these informal dynamics that operate in policymaking processes are a new phenomenon. Throughout the policymaking apparatus of government, collections of issue-conscious groups influence policy in a complex system of interrelationships. They have absconded with the sovereignty of "the people." Public policy studies and public administration theory are at a reckoning point; the democratic arbiter has been reduced to a quotation-mark-bracketed shell of a political sovereign ("the people").

The loop model, like a leaky bucket, fails to deliver the whole order. Public policy is subject to much more diffuse and multilateral influences than can be explained by the electoral democratic accountability loop. The name of the game is representation; yet symbolization has made off with the ball, the net, and the playing field.

Evidence That the Loop Model Is Mythical

Certain unpleasant realities of contemporary American political life place the electoral democratic accountability loop in doubt (see Pateman 1970). By the numbers:

1. The wants and needs of the people are, by and large, manipulated. There is no independent, popular will formation. News media, especially the electronic media from which most of the population gets its information, are managed more with an eye to entertain and titillate, to grab attention and sell air time to advertisers, than to politically inform.
2. Candidates for office rarely compete on the basis of complex policy alternatives. Image is much more important than substance. On campaign staffs, public relations gurus, advertising consultants, and style coaches are more important than policy analysts.
3. People do not vote for candidates on the basis of specific public policies, rationally considered. Majorities of the people often do not vote at all. Even if they did, a single-district, winner-

take-all, two-party electoral system is an extremely blunt instrument for registering the people's specific policy preferences
(Duverger 1954; Page and Brody 1972; and see Prewitt 1970,
on voters' ineffectiveness in municipal elections). It is highly
unlikely that a particular politician represents a particular con-
stituent across the entire panoply of complex issues facing the
nation. Single-issue voting further decreases the likelihood that
the daily votes of legislators are inspired by the discipline of the
electoral process. Those with more than one interest might get
what they want on abortion or gun control, but not on capital
gains or farm support. Indeed, it is mathematically impossible
for "the people" to be represented on the entire concatenation
of issues that affect their lives when choice is forced through
the binary centrist narrows of our electoral system.

4. After elections, coalitions of political entrepreneurs are more
   likely to be influenced by lobbyists, special interest associations, and close-knit policy communities; the pressure group
   system is bolstered by the politician-entrepreneur's need for
   campaign contributions, speaking honoraria, or well-funded ad
   campaigns (Blumenthal 1980). Nor does voting on the basis of
   party assure particular policy stances. Coalitions that do momentarily gel produce incoherent policy because they are con-
   trived contingently to attract a legislative majority. Ambiguous,
   contradictory, and confused mandates will then plague the bureaucracy as it tries to figure out *which* politically generated
   command to neutrally implement.

5. If eternal vigilance is the price of liberty, only radio talk show
   hosts seem willing to pay it. Americans frequently do not know
   their representatives' names, much less their positions and their
   policy successes or failures. Vigilance is a thirty-second TV spot
   excoriating opponents out of context.

6. It does not seem to matter that people are generally dissatisfied with the performance of Congress; they will still reelect
   their own members. Instead, calls for term limits resonate
   across the electorate.

The above examples are drawn from the sphere of national politics
in the United States, but we assert that most state and local politics

also fit the generalization. State and local electoral politics are virtually devoid of competition on specific policy initiatives. City council elections are fought over who is the best "family man." Many local governmental units in mass suburbia have been captured by various factions of real estate developer interests, if not by the local economic powerhouse.

Now, we do not want to be interpreted as asserting that because the loop leaks at every joint, and electoral politics is but symbolism removed from political events, that therefore there is no democratic accountability in the United States. We would not go quite that far in our critique. We do want to maintain that politics and public policy are subject to much more diffuse and multilateral influences than can be explained by the electoral democratic accountability loop. We also maintain that, along with the political insider influences rehearsed above, democracy flows from either side of the politics/administration dichotomy (which now should be thought of as a heuristic device). Robert Dahl (1971) and Charles Lindblom (1977) have insisted that this system be called *polyarchy* instead of *democracy*.

If policy directives do not flow in a direct channel from the people through elected officials, what of the otherwise unjustifiable top-down command structure that characterizes most public administration? This command-and-control apparatus has been imposed on public administration practice in the name of the sovereign people, but when the loop fails or is connected to interests other than the people, the command structure loses much of its reason for being. If the above analysis is even partly accurate, the people's name is being taken in vain.

The Folly of Binding Behavior by Writing Rules

The staying power of classical orthodoxy is attributable to its logical consistency and coherence. It is a tight interlocking system. So when Friedrich (1940) suggested the necessity of discretion, Finer (1940) objected that bureaucratic discretion is tantamount to the theft of popular sovereignty. When bureaucrats independently exercise governmental power, they are also independently defining the public interest, which only the people, through their elected representatives (the loop), have the right to do, in Finer's view. It followed that nonelected officials should be tightly controlled by an iron cage of rules, regulations, and standard operating procedures.

We have already seen the weaknesses of the loop, but even if it were fully operational, rules cannot work as Finer hoped they could. Four arguments may be adduced: (a) rules beget more rules; (b) the vagaries of language make it an inadequate instrument for precisely controlling bureaucratic behavior; (c) in many cases the more rules there are, the less they control behavior; and (d) externally generated rules are associated with dysfunctions such as gaming, goal displacement, creaming, and working to rule.

Policymakers and executives at the pinnacle of hierarchies typically exercise control via promulgation of rules. When subordinates' behaviors do not correspond to the original expectations, chiefs then pass down more rules as a corrective. Soon rules contradict one another, so clarifying rules are articulated, specified in more detail, and so on. But the human capacity to find loopholes or to be overly literal in interpreting commands will outrace management's ability to correct. Socrates said, "Such men are surely the most charming of all, setting down laws . . . always thinking they'll find some limit to wrongdoing . . . ignorant that they are really cutting off the heads of Hydra" (Plato, *Republic,* Book IV, 426e, cited in Fox and Cochran 1990).

Correspondingly, the more rules there are the more implementers must *choose* a particular concatenation of them to attend to. The paradigm case is the street-level police who work in a community with 200 years of encrusted ordinances. Enforcing the spitting-on-the-sidewalk ordinance may have to be neglected in favor of ridding the streets of drunk drivers and car thieves. In situations like welfare eligibility casework, there may be so many rules, regulations, and interpretations of them as to allow wide latitude to the personal quirks of particular caseworkers (see Lipsky 1980). Welfare policy will vary de facto from one county to the next (Riccucci 2005). The application of a rule to a case involves interpretation and judgment that are not specifiable (Beiner 1983).

Does all this mean there should be no rules? What about our cherished formula that we are a nation "governed by laws, not men"? An example from child rearing comes to mind. We get tied up in knots if we try to specify to our children complex codes of behavior. The best strategy seems to be to find the appropriate level of abstraction. "Be nice to your friends" works better than an infinite list of "don'ts" to cover every occasion. Inside the broad boundaries of the agreed standard, "be nice," there will be, alas, much discretion; reciprocal moral education will occur over its exercise.

But this is not the mainstream response to the crisis of democratic accountability called forth by the dysfunctions of representative democracy. Reform efforts presuppose the validity of precisely what is wrong.

Quixotic Mainstream Reforms

It is not as if the problems of the loop model of representative democracy have gone completely unnoticed by scholars and writers. The dominant tendency of those who recognize the problems, though, has been to reaffirm orthodoxy as an ideal and promote various reforms that might come closer to realizing the ideal. To the most influential of these writers—Mosher (1982) and Rosenbloom (2000) in public administration, Burke (1986) in public administration ethics, and Lowi (1969) in political science—the thought of abandoning legislative superiority based on popular sovereignty is . . . unthinkable. Lowi, in particular, has been critical of what he calls the second republic, which features legislatures relinquishing say-so to agency bureaucrats who then form unholy alliances with special interests in their regulatory purview. This demur founds the literature of iron triangles, agency capture, and policy communities. Lowi would return to the first republic, where the legislative branch reasserts its sovereign claims.

Such a stance suggests the need to search for institutional reforms that will put us on the path back to the legislative supremacy of the first republic. If representatives are insufficiently representative of their constituencies, then we need to make it easier for the constituents to vote (thus, passage of the "motor voter" law). If representatives use the power of their incumbency to garner disproportionate campaign war chests so that devious and venal media campaigns can be purchased, then we need campaign finance reform and term limitations. Reform's most likely result will be to relocate the loopholes, if the past is any guide. In sum, toying with procedural mechanisms seems to be a futile and quixotic exercise. Patching up leaks in one portion of the loop only increases the velocity squirting through others. Procedural maladjustments are symptoms of a more fundamental malady.

Halfhearted, crowd-/poll-pleasing pseudo-reforms on the politics side are exceeded by the same instinct on the administration side. A brief excursion into the currently fashionable tendency of outcomes measurement shows the difficulties of trying to reform the system when wearing the blinders of the loop understanding of democracy. The example in the next section represents an attempt to corral government by holding public servants to the norms of accountability, presumably bringing them under closer control by elected politicians and their political appointees. Such efforts are justified as exercises in popular sovereignty and democratic accountability. We want to display now the congruence between the loop model, which we disparage, and the attempt to make bureaucrats more accountable. To be wedded to the loop is to be unable to transcend Taylorist management styles. Starkly put, the loop model allows us to don the mantle of democracy only if we are dictators at the worksite. Obversely, to be democrats at the worksite is to steal sovereignty from the people. The illogic is most apparent in the recent emphasis on accountability.

Positivism in Public Administration

The Problem in Practice

In public administration practice, it is now more important to *show* you did your job than to actually *do* your job. The signifier has taken over the signified. This irony is the consequence of various attempts to measure performance, results, and outcomes.

This is the same irony that has recently caused the Broward County (Florida) sheriff to take responsibility for the crime reporting scandal associated with PowerTrac, a management accountability system that measured crime clearance rates. DeHaven-Smith and Jenne (2006) described this system as management by inquiry. The point of their article was "to explain the surprising efficacy" of the management system they were touting. But as it turns out, any conclusions about the program's success were premature. *Showing* crime rate reduction is something quite different from efficacy in crime reduction.

The system only appeared to be successful. As the state attorney's office alleged, "deputies made up confessions and pinned crimes on the wrong people" (McMahon 2006, B1). Several have admitted that the confessions they elicited were fabricated. In other words, the data were falsified. Pressure from higher-ups for a good "show" of crime reduction produced fertile conditions for gaming the system. Called into question here is the widespread wishful thinking about performance measurement as well as the entire family of evaluation and accountability methodologies that seem to have taken hold inside public institutions like some kind of mass delusion.

According to modern management theory, public administration can be improved by focusing on results. Hence, the managerial vocabulary of *performance budgeting*, *results-oriented management*, and *outcomes measurement* dominates the textbooks and the classrooms where rational managerialism is taught. Results-oriented government means that budgets and decisions are to be based on performance. Accordingly, the first administrative task is to develop performance indicators to measure outcomes. These indicators are intended to help legislators and managers focus on what results are to be expected from the funds allocated. The second task is to set target objectives so that progress toward them can be assessed. If the indicator measures, say, miles of highway laid, the target objective specifies how many miles of highway should be laid with the designated allocation of funds. But "miles of highway" is an inadequate indicator of the quality of the road or the difficulty of the terrain. Indicators lose utility if too much is read into them. For example, legislators who believe teacher salaries should be connected to student test score improvements have put more faith into this single indicator than is warranted by the indicator's validity. In this tidy test, they do not have the magical silver bullet.[1]

Attributing benefits or improvements to actual program activity is almost always problematic. Nonetheless, *performance measures* that do not quite measure what they are supposed to measure are dutifully developed by quiescent public servants.

Rather than taking stock of the performance and accomplishments of the agency, outcomes measurement and results-oriented management schemes can be intentionally falsified. Bogus or not, the "proof" does not report a reality so much as satisfy the needs of the higher-ups, who might be called upon to show that programs and operations under their supervision are efficient and effective. Never mind that outcomes could not be accurately measured in the first place. It all becomes a ruse, as those forced to participate in this game know too well. Reports that show magnificent results may appear impressive, but such reports corrupt the denotative meaning of the term *results*. In the process of outcomes measurement, all the meaningful symbols—performance, results, and outcomes—are debased. The ambiguity about government performance that was supposed to become transparent and unmistakable has spread; now the words themselves—performance, results, and outcomes—have become ambiguous (Beresford 2000).

The benefit derived from the public expenditure is, curiously, more hidden than before. The game is on. The target outcome is now framed in such a manner as to mask the absence of evidence of continuous improvement. Bogus performance indicators notwithstanding, the charade continues. Hapless bureaucrats blithely go through the motions of performance budgeting, program assessment, and outcome evaluation as commanded by central authority, which needs to show that government is being held accountable—according to the standards of positivists from academia who wrote the managerial prescriptions in the first place.

Government employees who work with these now-mutated symbols know what performance would mean in practice, but they cannot raise objections (until the prosecutor's office asks them to do so under oath). The system requires their subordination and quiescence. Their work is as meaningless as the symbols that describe it, but the *image* of accountability and performance is preserved. Those who know how to game the data have long suspected that the symbol "decreased crime rate" perhaps conceals a rising incidence of criminality instead.

Before it became known as a scandal, the PowerTrac system was implemented in a way that would please any rigorous modern management analyst or program evaluator. There were regular accountability sessions during which crime statistics were discussed, and sometimes areas for improvements were pinpointed. PowerTrac was "organized around formal meetings that interrogate managers about their decisions, actions, plans, and ideas" (DeHaven-Smith and Jenne 2006, 65). PowerTrac was an exemplar of the modern management genre. Its ambition for empirical, scientifically gathered evidence undermined its discursive potential. The system begins to eat its own tail as the desire for rational decision making generates irrational practices. This modern management style seemed to be working extraordinarily well—too well as it turned out. The Broward Sheriff's Office (BSO) was solving 45 percent of property crimes, compared to 18 percent nationwide. These incredible results were just that—lacking in credibility. Doubts arose. An inordinate number of crimes were cleared by exception (meaning that no arrest had been made). One deputy blamed five crimes on an individual who could not possibly have committed them all. But clearing five cases with one small lie must have seemed quite efficient at the time! Another deputy recalled how auto thefts were downgraded to burglaries, and burglaries to vandalism—hence creating a more pleasing show for consumers of PowerTrac information. The point of the game was always "show"—to show that one was doing one's job. The BSO example is well documented, but far from unusual.

Consider, too, the cheating scandal in the Houston Independent School District (HISD). Scores on reading and math tests led to investigations that demonstrated the teachers themselves helped students cheat on tests in order to "show" what a great job they were doing. And indeed, Wesley Elementary was featured on the Oprah Winfrey Show, and recognized by President Bush for its apparent improvements. The "Wesley way" of test-giving was to have teachers walk among the students during a test and stop next to those who had marked a wrong answer, and staying there until they marked the answer correctly. In another school, students were allowed to use this year's test (rather than last year's test) as a study guide for this year's test. Meanwhile, at Kashmere Gardens Elementary in HISD, the percentage of fourth graders who passed the reading and math portions of the standardized exam dropped from 100 percent to 17 percent in one year, once the cheating had been discovered and the principal reprimanded.

The Greater Alabama Council of the Boy Scouts also has experienced gamey performance reporting. By overstating membership, the group possibly received increased funding from organizations such as the United Way, according to National Public Radio (February 14, 2005). Later, Boy Scouts' overreporting of numbers of African American boy scouts came under suspicion as well.

The important scandal here is that reality has slipped away from the representation of it. Reality, it turns out, is exceedingly difficult to measure or represent. In public administration, the drive for empirical evidence mostly generates pressure for a good show amidst the atmospherics of accountability.

Performance symbols such as "crime rate reduction," or "test score improvement," or "membership increase" do not need reality as backup. The symbols are their own referents, the outcome of play of the game. In this way, managerialism betrays reality, vacating it of substance and inserting pleasant-sounding progress in its place. Image is the essence, the new reality.

Persistent Problems That Stem from Positivist Influence

The U.S. Office of Management and Budget (OMB) has recognized measurement problems in its 2003 publication "Performance Measurement Challenges" (U.S. OMB 2003). The OMB notes that several federal programs, totaling nearly $14 billion, are intended to help children learn to read. The measurement problem here is where to assign credit when reading indicators improve. Similarly, several federal programs provide student aid for low-income college students. Which one leads to the desired societal educational outcome is hard to demonstrate. Is it the largest, the Pell Grant program? Or is it the student loan programs? Outcomes may be difficult to measure, and when desired outcomes do take place, it may be that other programs contribute to the effect. Or it may be the state government's low tuition policy that is the causal variable —or none of the above. OMB also recognizes that results may not be achieved for many years. This is true of educational programs as well as space research.

A different measurement challenge arises when "the program relates to deterrence or prevention of specific behaviors" (U.S. OMB 2003, 10). Here, absence of data would be an indicator of success. A variation on this problem is provided by the OMB:

> A useful measure for the Coast Guard drug interdiction program could be the total volume of drugs entering the United States. This measure might be contrasted with drug seizure rates. High drug seizure rates might suggest that the Coast Guard interdiction strategies are effective. However, if the amount of drugs being sent rises significantly, and the number of seizures goes up to a lesser extent, the measure would still show that the Coast Guard program was effective, even though the volume of drugs getting through has increased substantially. (U.S. OMB 2003, 10)

A report by researchers in Canada spotted a difficult intangible operating in their studies (Townley, Cooper, and Oakes 2003). It seems that the more hope there is for a viable performance measurement system at the beginning, the more cynicism will be generated afterward. At a public agency in Alberta, Canada, the technologies of "new public management" (accountability reports, business plans, and performance measures) were put into place with the goal of "enhancing reasoned justification" for agency activities:

> We observed how managers in Alberta initially saw the Albertan version of New Public Management as promising opportunities for wider public consultation, and multiple arenas for dialogue and deliberation around issues of values, goals, and mission. All too often, however, attention shifted to technical inquiry, for example specific technologies for measuring performance, strategic planning, revising incentive mechanisms, costing outcomes, and linking budgets to results . . . . (1070)

As the measurement system was put into place, enthusiasm diminished. Professionals who were willing to become more accountable and accessible to a broader public were disappointed:

> Middle managers . . . increasingly saw these mechanisms as denying their expertise, closing off debate and promoting an instrumental rationalization. The operationalization of reasoned justification was undermined . . . The conditions for dialogic conversation and deliberative democracy . . . can all too easily degenerate into pseudo-participation and managerial manipulation of organizational commitments and identities . . . . (Townley, Cooper, and Oakers 2003, 1070)

The technology of performance assessment displaced concerns about dialogue, communicative action, public consultation, and openness. Amidst complex, disengaging systems of fake accountability, employees become alienated. Moral responsibility takes flight.

Adequate performance measures require a high level of detail, but on the other hand there are already too many measures, and too many evaluators who want yet another, and different, measure. In the era of intergovernmental, cross-agency networks, the centralizing tendency of performance assessment may seem especially out of place. In an environment of measurement chaos—and especially when gaming is known to be occurring—the usual solution is to reduce the discretion of the suspected miscreants and increase centralized control.

Within the foundationalist discourse known as *positivism*, challenging its rectitude is heresy. And such heresy is really not an empirical question; it is a question for political theory. As Waldo (1984, xxxi) said of positivism, "It is close to the mark to say that it is the political theory of those who seek to abolish political theory." Positivism's preoccupation with empirical data reveals an unwillingness to make itself definable in relation to other things; it wants to be the final arbiter of those other things. All signifiers in good standing are subject to the assessment: *That is an empirical question.*

Positivism is a metanarrative that continues to insist it is not a metanarrative. It is a politics that claims to be apolitical. Though the philosophers have abandoned most of its arguments, practitioners of positivism continue to believe, by virtue of their presuppositions, that their symbolizations (e.g., variables) provide a denotative link between language and reality; that positivism is capable, in a neutral manner, of capturing real things external to its symbolizations.

Signifiers in the positivist system do indeed refer to other signifiers in the same system. Like all linguistic systems, positivism, too, is a self-referential. We will attempt to redeem this claim using Karl Popper's famous doctrine of falsifiability.

Falsifiability

The term positivism continues to possess currency, but under more modest aspirations—that it can warrant falsifiability and description rather than verifiability and prediction. This empiricist-positivist discourse, forever altered by Karl Popper (1959), derived its antecedent meaning from the Vienna Circle's discourse on logical positivism—but as a significant rupture. Popper's shocking challenge to logical positivism's verification imperative (that only those statements that are empirically verified can be counted as true) resulted in the falsification theory. The current popularity of the notion of the null hypotheses is testimony to the persuasiveness of Popper's thinking in this regard. We cannot *prove* or *verify* a statement (contrary to the aspirations of the logical positivists), but we can *falsify* it. The more a statement endures repeated attempts to falsify it, the more that statement is accepted as true.

But even here, a niggling problem remains. Testing a hypothesis, even falsifying it, involves establishing whether or not the test that would falsify it is actually true or false: Is the falsifying test to be used a real and true one? At best, any test one might conjure has not yet been falsified —which does not make it valid. Popper had already taught us that claims such as "this test is the real and true test" could not be verified by experience or in any other empirical way. The upshot is that there is no *verified* test to be used infallibly for purposes of falsification. Hence, this matter of accepting one versus some other falsifying test as the real and true has no concrete foundation. Therefore, Popper's system is immanently unverifiable because the falsification move requires an empirical test that itself depends on verification that cannot be had. That is, the process of verifying facticity is implicitly disallowed by Popper's falsi-fication thesis. The upshot is that falsification theory, and the null hy-pothesis that represents it, preserves the verification thesis of logical positivism under the guise of dispensing with it. Even after Popper there is no viable philosophical justification for logical-deductive universal truth claims that attempt to reference empirical facts or objective real-ity. Even after Popper, the system is a self-referential one.

Even so and notwithstanding the contrary arguments, logical positiv-ism has hugely influenced the underlying values of social scientists, to which Herbert Simon's continued popularity attests. Research should be value-free, mathematical, logical-deductive in its postulates, and, some also claim, empirical. Much of the public administration literature, using utility-maximizing assumptions about human motivations borrowed from microeconomics, relies on the atomistic, self-interested individual as bed-rock truism. For example, rational choice theory is associated with math-ematical tools such as difference equations, queuing models, and probability estimation—tools intended to inform and assist policy analy-sis. In various ways, positivist social science proceeds apace, albeit with aspirations more modest than prediction and verification (naïve protocols of social science notwithstanding). Even though the heirs of logical posi-tivism abandoned, and in effect repudiated, the notion of scientific verifi-cation, the project of discovering truth based on scientific explanation of phenomena continues, and along with it the promise and pitfalls of cause-and-effect determinism, outcomes measurement, utility-maximizing in-dividuals, and instrumental rationality. Positivism, the perdurable metanarrative, continues to influence the contemporary debate over pub-lic administration practice. This is problematic in some important ways.

Perhaps it will be helpful to think of positivism as a style of dis-course, and forget the falsifiable mechanics of falsifiability. Let us think instead of the discourse as it appears in the public administration litera-ture. In this positivist discourse certain projects in public administration and public policy legitimate themselves as empirical exemplars. These would include *performance indicators*, *outcome measurement*, *results-oriented management*, and *performance budgeting*. Despite nuances and differences, there appears to be a certain outlook often referred to as *positivism* or *empiricism* or *realism* that underlies these public adminis-tration concepts. Within these discourses calling something an empiri-cal fact is a way of giving the claim associated with it a nice warm, hardy pat on the back. When we do it—and we have done it frequently in our duties as administrators (director of the School of Public Administration, or director of the Center for Public Administration)—we like to put all the facts in an Excel spreadsheet, which dresses them up in very quantitative, rational-look clothing that helps protect them against opposing claims and helps them survive the challenges that arise in group discussion. This is not an exercise in disingenuous fakery (although that is possible). If nothing else there is evidence that some sort of meditative contemplation of the issue at hand took place before the meeting. On practical grounds, we heartily endorse the strategic use of empirical facts, even if the strategy does not work as well in the social sciences as the natural sciences. We appreciate quantitative analysis, but an unyielding commitment to the empirical, as if it were some final arbiter of performance, accountability, or results leads to numerous practical problems in pubic administration.

Self-Referential Systems

The above critique of Popper's falsification is an immanent critique, within the logic of his own framework. There is an additional argument against falsification theory, with roots both within and outside of positivism's disciplined traditions. This argument is sometimes called sense-data atomism, or more derisively, the myth of the given, and more recently it has been called correspondence theory. The idea is that uncomplicated observation is adequate to the task of receiving information about the objective world. Moreover, it is felt that these sensory data impinge on human perception in distinct, uncomplicated, incorrigible micro-units of meaning. "Here, white, spherical, now" might confirm the hypothetical presence of a baseball. Sense data atomism has become known as the myth of given because such perceptions are, on closer examination, not so incorrigible after all. How could human perception, for instance, know that the object was spherical when one saw only one snapshot face of a round thing at the confirming moment? Worse, "here" implies elsewhere, "white" requires knowledge of color schemes, "now" requires a context of then and soon. In other words, humans have to be preprogrammed to report even the most elementary observing event. And, if preprogramming is required, how can the observation be the incorrigible confirmation? The link between reality-the-fact, on the one hand, and the word used to describe it, on the other, is a problematic connection. In various ways, various philosophers (Gödel [in Hofstadter 1999]; Wittgenstein 1953; Rorty 1979) have made the argument that symbols refer to other markers in the language system (or mathematics system in Gödel's case), not to external reality. Symbols refer not to external reality-in-itself, but to a system of signifiers that differ with respect to one another.

To cut to the chase, the implication of this line of argument is that so-called positivist or empirical research in the social sciences—including public administration mainstays such as survey research, outcome measurement, program evaluation, and policy analysis—may be regarded as self-referential epiphenomena. In their claims, all these require direct access to reality, unimpeded by language. But this cannot be had in philosophical discourse. In public administration in particular, reality-talk is always contextual, always taking place within a certain narrative using a particular linguistic system, be it democratic network governance, efficiency and effectiveness, or policy implementation. The political questions are about what to do, but the positivist discourse directs the conversation in a different direction.

Deconstructing the Loop Model

How many times have we heard someone at a conference, or in front of a class, or in a hallway conversation utter the mantra "That's an empirical question"? This mantra is a way of affirming the old logical positivist presupposition: the supposed correspondence between a term and the reality it refers to. The central assumption of mainstream social science—positivist or empirical—is that there exists such a correspondence, and that reality thus can be described. The worldview underlying this unexamined presupposition is both concealed and insinuated into the conversation with this splendid rhetorical maneuver: *That is an empirical question.*

But there are now some serious doubts about such a transcendent metaphysics. In an introduction of Jacques Derrida preceding a lecture at Stanford University, Rorty (1999) said:

> At the present time, however, the metaphysics of presence, the greatest imaginative achievement of the ancient world, remains the common sense of the West. Resistance to its overthrow, and ridicule of those who question it, are as predictable as were Athenian resistance to, and ridicule of, Socrates. But the heirs of Socrates have been expressing doubts

about Plato's metaphysics for a long time. Examples of such doubts are Hegel's historicism, Schiller's and Nietzsche's aestheticism, Dewey's pragmatism, Heidegger's revisionary account of Plato as a proto-Nietzschean, and Wittgenstein's and Davidson's treatment of language as a means for coordinating human action, rather than as a means of representing the non-human.

Positivism is the contemporary-usage word we are using to refer to the continued adherence to the representational, denotative use of language. What we are critiquing is a particular style of thought and practice that aspires for *empirical validation of generally true statements*. While the boundaries of this discourse are not precisely clear—no discourse has determinate and fixed boundaries—there is nonetheless an *œuvre,* as Foucault (1972, 24) calls it, that expresses the thoughts and experiences that operate on the discourse. And so the phrase "that is an empirical question" amounts to little more than a rhetorical flourish affirming the abundance of positivism. Similarly, phrases such as "God is great" or "May the Lord be with you" function to affirm the abundance of certain religious discourses—but with a different *œuvre,* or composition, or style. The importance of the invocation "that is an empirical question" should not be underestimated. It underscores the faith in provability. The operations, maneuvers, and images point us toward its object: empirical provability.

The discourse of positivism looks favorably upon empirical and causal exemplars. These would include *findings*, *observations*, *effects*, *determinants*, and *empirical assessment*. Deployment of these terms is a strategic move that appropriates an imagined final arbiter (empirical data about reality-in-itself) to aid a particular style of discourse in making encompassing generalizations.

The prestigious denotative moment is the representative one, where "reality-as-such" is *represented* by a word or symbol in some descriptive or explanatory sentence. In political democracies, the key moment is again a representative one (as in electoral representation) and the function is again to secure a final arbiter, this time for legitimate policy decision making. Our aim here is not to defeat this incredibly imaginative and successful strategy—that would be too bold an aspiration—but to describe it in a way that respects its powers and manifestations and maneuvers, on the one hand, and tries to imagine unconventional yet viable options, on the other. The first task, then, is to probe the denotative link that the word *representation* upholds.

Presence and Representation

Philosophers and epistemologists of late have been shying away from the idea that reality can be represented by human symbols, that there is a denotative foundation that could connect a human symbolic system (e.g., language or mathematics) to reality itself. Despite different connotations, representation in politics and representation in epistemology both implicitly promise to faithfully re-present something fundamental. Both kinds of representation promise to sustain a particular regime of authority. Jacques Derrida is among the more clear-sighted in critiquing this denotative promise.

When Derrida (1976) talked about the metaphysics of presence, he was referring to an attitude in Western culture that, among other things, favors speech over writing, an attitude he described as logocentrism. The purpose of writing, for the earlier linguist Ferdinand de Saussure, was to *represent* speech. Speech entailed face-to-face presence; writing entailed a relationship of *absence* between the author and the reader. Saussure's metaphysics of presence fuels an insistence that there is something immutable, something unchanging, natural, and real that humanity must heed: *presence.* "The concept of centered structure is in fact the concept of a freeplay based on a fundamental ground, a freeplay which is constituted upon a fundamental immobility and a reassuring certitude, which is itself beyond the reach of the freeplay. With this certitude anxiety can be mastered . . ." (Derrida 1980b, 280). Anxiety thus quelled by the fundament of presence, free play is expelled.[2] In the natural sciences this fixed presence that expels free play is called physical reality-in-itself. Before the advent of science, the ever-present presence and final arbiter was named God the father. Either way, natural or supernatural, the metaphysics allows presence to function as a source of authority, a presupposed reference to which all participants in the discourse defer.

For empiricists in public policy and public administration, the metaphysics of presence is derived from natural science metaphysics. [As the National Science Foundation (2005) says of political science proposals: "Research proposals are expected to be theoretically motivated, conceptually precise, methodologically rigorous, and empirically oriented."] The metaphysics of presence means realities of a certain type are known to exist; they are a priori present (pre-sent). The idea is that there is an empirical reality already out there, capable of settling disputes when we ask it the right questions in the right way. The status of the symbol in positivism is to represent that reality. That is to say, terms such as *fact*, *variable*, *indicator*, and *measure* promise faithful denotation of reality-as-such. The hidden premise behind positivism is this: whatever is most apparent to our consciousness, such as immediate sensory perception, is the most real as well as the most important.

Representation in a Symbolic System

In a representative political system, the citizen is the empirically verifiable unit of analysis. As a citizen, one is named and numbered. Illegal immigrants, on the other hand, are not empirically verifiable. The citizen, furthermore, is characterized by a *presence*, which is to say a body that physically must be somewhere, and accounted for when need be. The citizen, the person to be aggregated into the people when all are duly counted, provides the requisite (that is, apparent) link to reality-as-such. The presence of the body is self-evidently obvious to the eye, and it thereby grounds a symbolic system upon which both social science and democracy rely, with the fundamental unit of analysis being the individual. This potent combination yields a foundational presupposition that supports a powerful symbolic apparatus—the loop model of representative democracy. The ever-present assumption is that *this* symbolization system is grounded in something authoritative (not God in this case, but reality-as-such). Public administration/policy research protocols extend and elaborate this foundational premise through the many empirical studies that take for granted that the loop model works as advertised and that the people are sovereign.

Two Meanings of Representation

The key point of the loop model, for the purposes of the present section, is its endorsement and articulation of the representational system. This endorsement can now be seen at two levels simultaneously: an endorsement of the principle of political representation and an endorsement of the principle of empirical denotation. These endorsements are legitimating maneuvers. They reinforce each other, and in doing so disguise the radical *contingency* that characterizes the loop and shapes the polity defined by it. The loop, its representational presuppositions, and the things to which it refers (the people; embodied voters who are countable) are parts of a symbolic order whose symbolic free play is tethered to a foundation in order to pursue a grander claim: *The loop is a faithful manifestation of an empirically verifiable and truly democratic order.* Once the grander claim is acceded to, there are few grounds for disputing the legitimacy of public policy decisions that emanate from the loop. The function of public administration/policy research is to extend these premises and make them generalizable by colonizing competing metaphors.

Contingency

But progress toward this colonization is not inevitable. The empirically verifiable, truly democratic order—whereby the sovereign people make policy decisions via the loop model of democracy—generates immanent irrationalities. Loop decisions are not respectful of contingency, but must aspire to the universal and general. Democracy is made to be synonymous with standardization, universalism, and generality. Dewey's (1997) point in his 1909 essay on "The Influence of Darwinism on Philosophy" was that the important schism brought on by Darwin's thesis is not the much-publicized conflict between religion and science, but rather a conflict within the scientific discourse. Scholarly discourse, before Darwin, had idealistically subscribed to purposeful "grand design" formulations of nature. Secondly, wrote Dewey (15–16), "the classic type of logic inevitably set philosophy upon proving that life *must* have certain qualities and values. . . . The duty of wholesale justification inevitably accompanies all thinking that makes the meaning of special occurrences depend upon something that once and for all lies behind them. . . . It turns thought to the business of finding a wholesale transcendent remedy. . . ." The universalizing, generalizing, abstract form of philosophy suffered a severe blow from Darwin's contingency thesis. Chance, accident, environmental circumstances, and "the specific conditions of generation" were elements of a new logic that Dewey saw displacing the previous philosophical project, whose questions dissolved in the face of Darwinian contingency. Positivism's demand for systematization, generalizability, and universality is part of the package that Dewey recognized as pre-Darwin classic philosophy.

Symbolic Colonization

Meanwhile, representation's desire to be something more than symbolism —to claim the status of denotation—is a gambit that overreaches. "The people" wants to deny it is a symbol and additionally insists that it can be represented and empirically verified. The individual bodies of the voters are factual proof of the presence of the individual, aggregable into "the people" via counting protocols, both electoral and administrative. The political and administrative counting of individuals is how proof that "of the people" is demonstrated. The loop does not admit that it is a system of symbolizations, and positivist public administration/policy research assists in this denial; and in doing so downplays the importance of contingency in human affairs.

Other legitimating systems have used other symbolic orders to accomplish much the same thing—the divine right of kings comes to mind—and none of them seem to want to acknowledge their contingency, transience, and cultural particularity. They all want to do what "the people" wants to do: generalize, systematize, and universalize. As empirical discourse, "the people" wants to colonize all other symbolizations. A contingent symbolic order is asserted as the natural (or divinely inspired) order. To put it another way, a particular metaphor assigns itself the task of regulating all metaphors, hence becoming *the Metaphor. The people* wants to be that *metaphor*, with the loop and its attendant institutions thereby enlisted to enforce that regime of truth and democracy.

Devotion to the *metaphor* that regulates all metaphors amounts to a colonization of the terrain of other metaphors. *The people* or *God* or *Allah* present themselves as the *metaphor of presence,* as the arbiter. Yet they are contingent metaphors, relying on stable yet malleable cultural practices and conditions, on variations in practice and meaning from one setting to the next, and on media speed in assimilating/defeating metaphorical competitors. Whether it is named the *common good, the public interest*, or *the people*, the big-M Metaphor, like *God*, aspires to be the metaphor-regulating Metaphor. The role of public policy analysis and public administration in the loop metaphor is to expand the reach and scope of the loop, and thereby of *the people*. Linguistic hegemony does not a democracy make.

Symbols and Environment

If we listen to Mosca (1939) there is no avoiding such domination. Is a culture-wide, symbolic order inherently hegemonic and expansionist? If hegemony implies purposefulness, the answer may be no. Dominance can come about by accident. If the reader will allow us a

Darwinian metaphor, we would say that symbolizations evolve and adapt to their environments, which are made up of other symbolizations. This does not require teleology or purposeful intent; accident is all that is needed. It only retrospectively seems that each species (or symbolization) had a purposive survival strategy. In the words of Dewey (1997, 9–10) "the classic notion of species carried with it the idea of purpose. . . . Since this purposive regulation is not visible to the senses, it follows that it must be an ideal or rational force." While Dewey's criticism of teleology in biology and philosophy was astute, I do not believe it occurred to him that the evolution of human symbolizations can be as contingent, irrational, and accidental as biological evolution. As Robert Burns famously put it in 1785, "The best-laid schemes o' mice an' men gang aft agley" (from the poem "To a Mouse, on Turning Up Her Nest With the Plough").

And so, what Foucault calls the *episteme* is but the *knowledge order* that turned out to be the dominant one. So we "citizens" must learn to speak the language of its symbolizations, we must submit ourselves as countable bodies, we must verify the physical reality of our factual bodies, and thereby affirm the Metaphor under which we are all represented.

But now, empirical individuals no longer add up to the people. The insecurity brought about by the free play of signifiers has been named. The need for foundations has been deconstructed as pathos, driven by a foundation-desiring anxiety.

The scandal in all of this for public administration is that empirical reality, and with it democracy, have slipped away from the representation of it. Reality and democracy, it turns out, are exceedingly difficult to measure or represent. Instead, the drive for empirical evidence narrows the scope of attention in public administration and generates pressure for a good show of data amidst the atmospherics of accountability and bogus power structures supposedly derived from the people.

Symbols Unmoored

The crux of our argument is that the era of foundations is over. Representation no longer works smoothly because the foundational anchor between the symbol and the thing the symbol is supposed to denote has been loosed. Thus unmoored from foundations, symbols play freely with one another. The symbolic order, in the absence of foundational presence, is all there is with which to discipline the symbolic order.

So we will not propose a new utopia based on a new foundation. Mostly, we expect to have the same symbolic order—malleable though it will be—at the end of the book as at the beginning. Indeed, we are rather fondly attached to those aspects of the symbolic order that reflect *reason,* and we would be reluctant to displace such with supernaturalism or religious mystification. But reason should not fool itself about its universality, its generalizability, or its empirical foundations. Reason's next step, it seems to us, would be to find a way to accommodate the random, the accident, the uncertain, and the nonuniversal moment. Reason should find a way to embrace contingency. Public administration/policy researchers claiming that different inputs yield different outputs is perhaps a weak way of honoring contingency, but maybe it is a start.

In this chapter we have problematized representation rather than presupposing it; we have revealed as malleable the foundations of the representative democratic accountability feedback loop. In the process we have begun to understand symbols not as object representations, but as something potentially more important than that—a topic to be revisited in chapter 5. Meanwhile, the continued pretension that positivist protocols will make public administration more accountable to its democratic masters yields up absurdity and irrationality. And we are not the only ones to recognize that something is amiss between democracy and public administration. In the next chapter we will take a look at three proposals that challenge orthodox public administration.

Notes

1. In Florida the name of this test is FCAT, the results of which determine whether a student will receive a high school diploma and whether a school is fully funded the next year. Kelly Services is the company that won the contract to score the essay questions, and advertised to hire 300 part-time employees to do so, at $10 per hour (Kleindienst 2006.) Meanwhile, the College Board admitted that it misreported scores of 4,000 students who took the SAT exam in October 2005 (Arenson 2006).

2. By free play, we mean that symbols (words, signifiers, images) are not *necessarily* fixed to a foundational, denotative meaning. For example, rock is not necessarily a reference to the hard object in the garden. It might also be a form of guitar music or perhaps the gentle sway of a porch swing or chair. And with free play, it might also be spelled roc or wrok. Foundational, denotative fixed meanings delimit such free play.

2

Alternatives to Orthodoxy

Despite the manifest flaws in the loop model of American governance, most calls for reform presuppose the efficacy of the loop model. The incredulity of representative democracy is both a curse and an opportunity. It is a curse on public administration because it deprives it of direct access to popular sovereignty as it is popularly understood. Public administrators' political masters sometimes exhibit behaviors associated with charlatans and demagogues, and sometimes crooks, parading under the garish banner of the will of the people. The intellectual misgivings associated with representative democracy provide an opportunity to theorize anew.

The three dominant responses to this paradigm anxiety have been neoliberalism, constitutionalism, and citizen activation. All owe their respective structures to the requirements of legitimacy and accountability. The most highly successful alternative model, named *neoliberalism* to gather in its variety of iterations (privatization, reinventing government, new public management, and others) will be discussed in the first section below. This first alternative to orthodoxy replaces the rule-bound, hierarchical, and sometimes inefficient bureaucracy with market reforms. Here we do not worry so much about following rules, but instead focus on outcomes, results, and performance. We end the section on neoliberalism by noting that it is open to corruption, unreasonably relies on social science methodology that cannot perform its assigned tasks, and displaces values such as democracy, openness, fairness, and equity with an intensified and toxic instrumental rationality.

The second alternative substitutes the Constitution for the electoral victors of the moment. Here loyalty to the sovereign people need not be compromised if it can be shown that constitutional principles have primacy over the merely elected. From the motley crew shouting conflicting orders, we may choose which ones to obey when guided by the constitutional founding. *Constitutionalism*, as developed in the Blacksburg Manifesto (see Wamsley et al. 1990, for the published version), is the topic of the second section below. This body of discretionist thought is a reaction to the bureaucrat bashing that began in the 1970s. If the loop fails to deliver sensible manifestations of popular will, administrators can turn to the Constitution for legitimacy and guidance. We conclude the second section by arguing that constitutionalism is an insufficiently radical departure from orthodoxy because it attempts to assign constitutional legitimacy to the extant administrative state, with all its flaws.

More to our liking is the third alternative, the *communitarian* tendency, which seeks to replace the loop with direct interface between administration and the citizenry. The third alternative seeks to bypass the electoral loop by going directly to the sovereign citizens. Here we are instructed to replace electoral, representative, weak democracy with direct, strong democracy. But by embracing the entire citizenry, on the one hand, and regarding all issues as public policy issues, on the other, the communitarian ideal founders. But first, neoliberalism.

Neoliberalism

Neoliberalism may be considered an extension of conventional liberal-utilitarian thought in that the individual comes before the community, and community is or ought to be the realm of economic activity, wherein the role of the state is to keep peace in this community marketplace. "The internal design of the relation between the 'natural' private realm of the market and the 'artificial' public realm of the state has been the object of constant elaboration and adjustment" (Pesch 2003, 53). This is the background theme of several reform efforts in public administration that we gather together for critique under the umbrella of neoliberalism.

Privatization, Contracting Out, and Performance Assessment

The reform efforts that have gone by the names *public choice*, *privatization*, *reinventing government*, and *new public management* are examples of a genre that promises reform and radical change in the way the public sector is run. This genre of managerialism picked up steam in the Reagan administration in the United States, the Thatcher administration in Britain, and in Australia in the 1990s. There is the promise of less red tape, and an emphasis on performance and effectiveness rather than rules. "Reformers sought to replace authority and rigidity with flexibility; the traditional preoccupation with structure with improvements to process; and the comfortable stability of government agencies and budgets with market-style competition" (Kettl 1997, 447). Though Kettl writes in the past tense, and others would argue that any or all of these iterations of reform are by now passé, the pressure continues, at least in the English-speaking world, for public administrators to introduce or extend the practices of contracting-out and to adopt performance-measurement reforms. Efficiency is valued highly in the school of thought we are calling neoliberalism. Discourse that, in contexts other than neoliberalism, would be appreciated as a form of democratic deliberation, are regarded here as a transaction cost that preempts other opportunities (Horn 1995). These styles, which we gather into the genre of neoliberal reform, challenge the orthodox model in some ways (the rules orientation of orthodoxy is not heeded with the same respect), but in other ways (rationalism and scientism) neoliberalism reiterates and affirms the presuppositions of orthodoxy.

The term *liberal* has become a mutant metaphor that, when mentioned by certain right-wing talk-show hosts, is hissed with a snarl on the lips rather than spoken in a normal tone of voice. This may seem odd, because a classical liberal might find herself ideologically close to those in the United States who nowadays are identified as neoconservatives or probusiness right-wingers. This is not so much irony as custom. In the United States, the image of a liberal is someone who supports the welfare state, including Social Security, public education, some kind of nationalized health care system, as well as "big government," civil rights, and equal opportunity regardless of race or ethnicity. In Canada and Japan, on the other hand, the Liberal Party has always been linked closely to business interests, retaining the classical libertarian meaning of the term liberal.

The lineage of neoliberalism is not New Deal or Great Society liberalism, but classical liberalism, by which the government restrains itself from interfering in business, science, scholarship, and religion to the extent possible. In its reaction against the "excessive government" of the New Deal, the Chicago School of Economics has been identified by Foucault (1994b, 79) as an expression of American neoliberalism, which "seeks to extend the rationality of the market, the schemes of analysis it proposes, and the decision making criteria it suggests to areas that are not exclusively or not primarily economic." While classical liberalism placed much emphasis on the rule of law and constitutional guarantees, neoliberalism expresses an ideological standpoint favoring market-system solutions and methods over government intervention—especially when it comes to restrictions on business operations, corporations, and the flow of capital. Jeremy Bentham's Panopticon writings, which offered an interventionist social-engineering twist to his utilitarian liberalism, along with Adam Smith's advocacy of markets in *Wealth of Nations*, provide the most relevant lineage from classical liberalism to neoliberalism.[1] The attacks on government beginning in the 1970s, and on bureaucracy in particular, can be traced significantly to neoliberal advocacy of limited government—limited spending, limited taxation, limited regulation, and limited interference in free enterprise. Market systems have demonstrated themselves superior to centralized government planning systems (Lindblom 2001), and so neoliberal philosophy has commanded significant power and influence over the affairs of nations, states, and communities.

Government is put to best use, in the neoliberal frame, by making markets available to free enterprise. This use of government may range from international free trade agreements to engaging in war to promote "freedom." Government under the influence of neoliberalism enables the exploitation of resources, including labor and raw materials, in an efficient and effective manner. Governmental interventions to accomplish these political-economic tasks are not as limited as they would have been in the classical liberalism that John Locke, David Hume, or Edmund Burke envisioned. Classical liberalism would abhor proposals to take people's private homes or businesses and hand that property over to a corporation that would spur economic development. But the 2005 U.S. Supreme Court ruling in *Kelo v. City of New London, Connecticut* allowed government to use eminent domain to transfer private property to another private interest in hopes of boosting the tax base. Proponents of classical liberalism probably would not even list old-style takings—limited to those that involve public purposes such as new roads or schools—high on the action agenda. The new use of eminent domain power signals the more aggressive corporate style of neoliberalism, and it is a global as well as a local phenomenon. Hence neoliberalism and globalization are often mentioned in the same sentence. With neoliberalism, strong and powerful governments armed with mighty military capacity and supported by international financial institutions are deployed to make the world safe for free enterprise. This top-down expression of institutional power has the potential for undermining both democratically elected governments and tyrannical despots.

Neoliberalism is criticized for helping to create a race to the bottom, as corporations move operations to places with the least restrictive environmental laws, the weakest labor standards, and the cheapest natural resources. Inequality in wealth and power thus increases when policy is guided by neoliberal philosophy (Pollin 2005).

Neoliberalism as a domestic political movement is all about downsizing government, privatizing government-run operations to the extent possible, and "getting government off our backs," as the late U.S. president Ronald Reagan was fond of saying. By that he meant the deregulation of business—a thrust much appreciated by businesses large and small, which frequently found themselves tied down by government red tape. The metaphors deployed in trying to improve public management are borrowed from business models. For example, the metaphor "customer service" was an attempt to get public managers to deploy a business frame of mind in the way that it related to citizens. Thompson's (2003) association of orthodox public administration to "the Prussian model" indicates how neoliberalism can be seen as a significant challenge to orthodoxy:

> In the US the progressive movement created modern public administration. To a remarkable degree the progressive reforms—an executive, input-oriented budget, a professional civil service and merit-based public personnel administration, control by rules, standardization of procedures, task specialization, and a strict administrative hierarchy, with clearly delineated staff and line functions—were based on the Prussian model. . . . One of the best-known apologies for this practice was Woodrow Wilson's argument that politics and administration are different functions, making it possible to borrow administrative practices from an authoritarian state without thereby threatening democratic politics—"If I see a murderous fellow cleverly sharpening his knife . . . ." (333)

Government, because it is rule-bound rather than market-sensitive, was seen as unable to operate enterprises that require flexibility and adaptability. In public administration, neoliberalism translates into a desire for transparency on the one hand, and dismantling of governmental regulations on the other. At issue is the implementation of regulations that seem to lack consistency and efficiency. It is better to limit government to supplying public goods, say the public choice advocates who have strongly influenced neoliberal economic theory.

Neoliberals are not unambiguously antigovernment, however. Some of them, at least, have taken it upon themselves to try to improve public-sector management. According to Thompson (2003, 334): "Old style bureaucracy is authoritarian and hierarchical, those attributes never comported well with democratic values. Moreover, the requirements of directing giant, vertically integrated, functional organizations has tended to overwhelm the capacity of the public and its elected representatives to attend to the general welfare. Limiting the scope of the public sector to the provision of services that truly are infused with the common interest cannot but enhance the efficacy of democratic governance mechanisms."

Economic theories of organization and management, especially emanating from public-choice-style political economy, helped buttress the case for reform. Privatization, downsizing, load-shedding, and contracting-out were pursued with the purposes of making government smaller. Keen attention was paid to the incentives of institutional practices; those that lead to desired results were continued or strengthened. Otherwise, the incentive system needed to be changed. Principal agent theory, performance assessment, and a focus on measurement of results and effects were aimed at making government more efficient and effective. Even nonprofit organizations are advised to adopt neoliberalism's instrumental rationality, as when Peter Drucker famously warned the Girl Scouts that their benefactors would judge them on the basis of results. If success is to be measured by effects, then it became imperative that government adopt the methods of empirical social science, whereby indicators of performance could be reported to political authorities to verify programmatic veracity.

Hence, neoliberalism as expressed in the public administration literature is laden with calls for systematic analysis and for adoption of the habits and techniques of policy analysis (Barzelay 2001). The emphasis on technology and the transfer of technology that could be found in neoliberalism was reiterated in public administration as an emphasis on analytical techniques (Lynn 1996).

At the same time, centrally managed institutional rules and routines were to yield to "situation specific requirements of policy entrepreneurship" (Barzelay 2001, 158). In some attempts at implementing the neoliberal managerial program, this was to be accompanied by individualized performance contracts rather than traditional civil service rules. Indeed, the tremendous emphasis on outcomes assessment, performance measurement, and program evaluation may signal the limits of neoliberal managerialism. The ever-greater specification of performance goals and output measures (Kettl 1997) mirrors the problematic we described in chapter 1.

Critique of Neoliberalism

Reservations about neoliberalism and its business-oriented methods have gained increasing expression in public administration journals. "[R]unning government like a business means that public managers increasingly regard the public as customers to be served rather than as citizens who govern themselves through collective discourse practices" (Box 1999, 22). Indeed, there are some very good reasons to be skeptical of neoliberal managerialism, not the least of which are: (1) the potential for corruption and (2) the unrealizable ambitions regarding performance measurement and outcome assessment.

Corruption

Certain private-sector aspects of neoliberal managerialism have been linked to corrupt practices. Proponents of privatization, for example, "ignore impressive examples of inefficiency, waste and corruption in the American experience with defense, construction projects, and health care—all mostly produced privately with public dollars" (Morgan and England 1988, 979). Names have been given to various scurrilous or circumstantial yet common practices: low-balling, buying-in, cost over-runs, collusive bidding, unforeseen circumstances, or market failure (Miller and Simmons 1998). One should not expect free competition when there are numerous examples of single-bid contracts, negotiated bids, wired deals, outright bribery, and "profit"-sharing kick-back schemes for anyone who reads newspapers to know about.

The concern among neoliberals has more to do with slacker employees than with the inevitable corruption that contracting-out yields. While neoliberalism is keen to reduce the power of public-sector labor unions, contracting-out can result in reduced health care benefits for workers, lower wages, and pernicious work rules. Yet, the most enduring and contentious debates are in the areas of contract oversight and corruption, as Leonard White long ago reported. "During the 1870's there was both incompetence and dishonesty in the large custom houses: discipline and integrity among the navy-yard labor forces were at low ebb; the Indian service had been roundly condemned by Garfield; land agents connived at irregularities, and surveyors made fraudulent claims for work not performed" (1958, 367).

Corruption notwithstanding, the more contracting out, the more resources necessarily will be devoted to contract writing, specification of standards, performance monitoring, and auditing. The promulgation of rules by which procurement policies are implemented likewise will be necessary. In addition to providing a new outlet for red tape, another layer of accountability and oversight bureaucracy will be necessitated.

The Problems of Measurement and Causal Attribution

Public-sector problems are often the most difficult to solve, much less define. That is to say, there often is not a political consensus on what to do, and there is not the technical expertise to solve the problem even if the what-to-do problem were solved. Multiple values and perspectives come into play. In this sort of turbulent environment, the hope that performance measurement will be of any use whatsoever is a hope for too much. The problem is not only one of constructing indicators that are valid, but of deciding what category of thing to count. "Infant mortality rate," for example, a widely used indicator of a population's access to health care, is controversial when used that way. But that is among the least controversial environmental and public health indices. Should asthma be used as a national health indicator? Such a national standard would be opposed by smoke-stack industries.

An additional difficulty comes when attributing causality to governmental programs. Was it state and federal environmental programs that caused the air and water quality improvements in Michigan? Or was the "cause" the fact that so many manufacturing facilities were relocated to union-free states or low-wage countries during the same time period?

In practice, there are numerous problems with performance indicators. On this score, the critique of orthodoxy presented in chapter 1 applies to neoliberalism in spades, because accountability via social science techniques has become an integral part of neoliberal social engineering.

Among the most important difficulties with the use of social science techniques is the matter of gaming the system. Gaming implies that presumably stable indicators are incorporated into policy. Getting arrested criminals to admit to crimes they never committed, or helping students cheat on standardized exams are but two ways of gaming the system. If standardized education assessments test only for mathematics competencies, teachers will stop teaching art and citizenship. If a job training program rewards a job placement agency or counselor according to the proportion of registrants that find jobs, there is an incentive to register for training only those who are likely to get jobs. Gaming is measure specific.

Reports of the irrationality of rationalistic performance measures abound. "Consider the case of chandeliers [in the former Soviet Union]. . . . Because the original production description chosen was weight, the Soviets could soon boast the heaviest chandeliers in the world" (Courty and Marschke 2003, 269). And one can imagine the absurd scenario playing out in full. If performance measures in the nail-making industry emphasized quantity, one can be assured that the nails will be too small to hold the chandeliers in place in the ceiling. And if quality indicators of light bulbs focus overmuch on luminescence, every chandelier is also likely to be a fire hazard.

Meanwhile, evaluators can also game the system, by making themselves seem indispensable. A particularly wicked strategy would be to create as many different and complicated indicators as possible. Everyone is confused except the evaluator!

In sum, the proposition that performance can be reduced to variables that can be measured, and that outcomes, results, effects, and even non-events can be attributed to programs and policies, amounts to fanciful faith in what social science methodology can accomplish.

Neoliberal Extremism

Neoliberal reform, in its public management manifestations, has been labeled "a remarkable revolution" (Kettl 1997, 1). It has challenged orthodoxy in important ways, yet some things remain the same. Neoliberalism's reliance on principal agent theory (which informs the rationale for contracting out) reiterates the politics-administration dichotomy. "[P]rincipal-agent theory is especially applicable in the public sector, where the relationships between citizens (principals) and politicians (their agents) and between politicians (principals in this case) and bureaucrats (their agents) are a constant source of fascination" (Box 1999, 28). The idea is that agents can be fired by their principals if their performance assessments do not indicate efficiency or effectiveness. But efficiency and effectiveness are sometimes construed in peculiar ways. The sacking of Amtrak's president David Gunn is a case in point.

Referred to as the best president in years of the nation's only passenger railroad by the *New York Times* (November 10, 2005, A30), the editorial noted that the U.S. Senate "managed to get a 93–to-6 vote to authorize $11.6 billion for passenger rail service in the next six years—as close to an all-out endorsement of Amtrak as you can get." But the Board of Directors wanted competition, outsourcing, load-shedding of certain corridors, free-market modes of transportation, and expense cutting—perhaps even liquidation of Amtrak. These reforms have a constituency and an argument—Amtrak's service needs improvement and its control of train tracks and train stations should be opened up to competition (perhaps from certain legislators' important campaign contributors). Neoliberalism's managerial reforms sometimes look a lot like orthodoxy, even as they impose a harsher set of economic utility-maximizing assumptions. And in spite of the genre's antihierarchy rhetoric (e.g., see Thompson 2003), organizational control remains vertical and severe. At the same time, bureaucracy's cultural signature, instrumental rationality, is insinuated into the public discourse with increased fervor, driving out values such as fairness and equity, as well as fraternity, liberty, and equality.

Neoliberal ideologues have gone to extremes to advance privatization even when corporations have no useful role to play. In a proposal by one senator, the National Weather Service would have had to limit the weather information they make directly available to the public so that weather information would have to be funneled through private corporations instead (Krugman 2005). Requiring anyone who wants Medicare drug benefits to enroll in a corporate-provided plan has increased not only administrative costs but has caused former Miami Dolphins coach Don Shula to go on TV and tout the benefits of enrolling in the drug plan that pays him to go on TV. Meanwhile, the same law explicitly prohibits Medicare from using its clout to negotiate better deals for the consumer/citizen/taxpayer (Krugman 2005).

In one of the more startling critiques of neoliberal managerialism, Imas (2005) reconstructed the management discourse in Chile in the

1970s. Imas argues that Chile became a rational management society due to colonization, and that "because Chile was the result of imported ideas, lives and cultures, Chileans did not have a strong historical identity. Therefore, they were susceptible to foreign discourses, such as rational management" (113). Moreover, unequal control of mines, farms, and natural resources had, by the 1960s, exacerbated serious class divisions in the country and created a confrontational environment. Salvador Allende was elected president in 1970 by a left-wing coalition; by 1973 the right wing had him assassinated and "Chile was to be re-born as a modern rational organization, and a previously somber and insignificant figure of its history was to be catapulted to a central role: rational management emerged to write the new Chile" (119). Imas's chilling first-person account of the day Salvador Allende was assassinated— September 11, 1973—conveys the terror, dismay, and anxiety of not knowing the whereabouts of his father (who "disappeared" at the National Stadium).

It is important to remember that a new era had arrived in Chile. Before Allende, Chile was run like a big *hacienda;* after the military coup of 1973, Chileans learned a new model of organization and a new model of man (Imas 2005). "These market principles insisted on the right to private property, the non-interventionist nature of the state and the domination of market forces through privatization and liberalization of the economy . . . Moreover, under this new organization, all vestiges of bureaucratic political rule (as they referred to democracy) and Chilean history would simply disappear as if they never existed" (Imas 2005, 124). Imas's story, then, is about a Chile that acquired a new historical identity and came to resemble a rationally organized society guided by technocratic and rational managers. Its previous identity had been "disappeared."

The Chilean example underscores the unavoidable political backdrop of rational managerialism, which is still regarded in some circles as a neutral force. Institutions are, above all, routinized relations of power (as we will argue more fully in chapter 4). Public administration theories that posit an administration that is separate from politics fail to convey the everyday, relational practices of power. Neoliberal reform pushes forth a one-dimensional instrumental rationality and seems unwilling or unable to abide multidimensional value plurality. This one-dimensionality endorses *limited* government, but neoliberal proponents of *effective* government are harder to find.

In contrast to neoliberalism, the next two models may be considered discretionist (Fox and Cochran 1990) and are therefore willing to acknowledge the inevitably political component of actions and events that concern public administration. As we shall see, these models affirm a proactive public administration on behalf of the public interest. Administrative discretion, in turn, is based explicitly or implicitly on the incredulity of representative democracy as we know it (called weak democracy by Adams et al. 1990; known also as overhead democracy and unilateralism in Mosher 1982). All discretionist views imply skepticism toward contemporary political authority.[2] Although discretionists dismiss the politics-administration dichotomy, they also would like to leave behind the petty bickering, grandstanding, and gridlock that stem from partisan politics.

The Constitutionalist Alternative

Constitutionalism means different things in different contexts and literatures. Here the term is used to identify a class of arguments now sufficiently solidified and complete to qualify as an alternative theory vying to replace orthodoxy in public administration. The leading intellectual proponent of constitutionalism in this sense is John Rohr. His case for refounding public administration based on a particular reading of the founding is all the more influential as the cornerstone of the Blacksburg Manifesto (Wamsley 1990, 23) and as the template for various interpretations from D. F. Morgan (1990) to Spicer and Terry (1993). As the impressively erudite Rohr is an unlikely man of straw, it is Rohr's (1986) argument that merits explication and critique.

Rohr's Thesis

Rohr is straightforward: "The purpose of this book is to legitimate the administrative state in terms of constitutional principle" (Rohr 1986, ix). But how can the Public Administration (capitalized here to reflect the convention of Blacksburg scholars) be a constitutionally legitimate governmental structure in its own right when the word *administration* appears nowhere in the written Constitution? Rohr's answer is that a constitution is more than the particular contract that the document codifies. A constitution is a covenant (x). Given the religious overtones of *covenant*, Rohr here seems to mean that a contract is the letter, whereas a covenant is the spirit, of an agreement between two or more parties. But how may one "read" the spirit? Rohr's answer is that it should be read through the exegesis of writings of those engaged in the argument (9), exegesis being the critical interpretation of text. For Rohr, this exegesis has as its object an expanded text, including the actual Constitution, *The Federalist Papers*, and writings of the antifederalists as well. The purpose of exegesis is to distill larger, more fundamental verities from the clutter of impassioned points made by debaters in the heat of the moment. In such a context, the constitutional document itself is only the provisional synthesis, a strong but not decisive point held in tension in the larger agonistic web of argumentation and counterargument.

Constitutional in this sense is certainly a more encompassing concept than the crabbed Constitution of the strict constructionist jurist. Constitutionalism as a legitimizing font for the administrative state is really about the founding. "The Constitution is the symbol of the founding of the Republic and in politics, 'foundings' are normative" (Rohr 1986, 7). "The source of authority of regimes is the founding act itself" (179).[3] But what is *founding?* In the history of political philosophy, many watershed thinkers revere foundings. To Plato, for instance, if the ideal of the Republic cannot be actualized, the second best state is one of laws stemming from a founding. Similarly, Rousseau settles for the founding acts of a legislator, failing the emergence of institutional manifestations of the general will. Social contract theory in general—Hobbes, Locke, and, recently, Rawls—imagines some founding moment when for various reasons the people come together to create unabrogatable arrangements for living together in (at least) peace, if not justice and harmony. Rohr suggests that this second-best historicism is what he has in mind. By such logic, foundings may approximate to varying degrees Absolute Justice/Truth. Although they are a compromise from Absolute Justice, and they differ from place to place and time to time (such differences already a regrettable move along the spectrum from ideal to appearance), these approximations usually depend on the sagacity of the humans (or suffer from the lack thereof) who serve as the vehicles of Truth or Justice. In the case of the founding of the American republic, though, there is not one wise Solomon-like lawmaker; there is instead a formidable committee whose members argue.

Rohr's innovation, then, is to embody the founding, not in a founder, nor even in the founding fathers, but rather in the thoughts and principles flowing between the participants and between them and their interlocutors. "The founding was in the argument" (1986, 179). Thus, when we swear an oath to protect the Constitution, we swear to honor the founding and the tradition coalesced by that act, we swear to honor the argument, and in a sense we swear also to engage ourselves in the argument, bounded by the high principles through which it was originally conducted.[4]

So how is all this founding talk related to public administration? Rohr (1986) makes three modest claims: "The administrative state is consistent with the Constitution, fulfills its design, and heals a longstanding major defect" (13). First, although public administration exercises executive, legislative, and judicial powers, it does not violate the relaxed standard of separation of powers, which standard may be adduced from the founding argument. Second, public administration provides a constitutional "balance wheel," a function originally assigned to the non-elected Senate. Third, public administration provides a measure of (demographic) representation insufficiently fulfilled by the strictly constitutional branches.

Critique of Constitutionalism

We have tried to portray constitutionalism with the genuine sympathy we feel for it and the cause that it champions. Constitutional legitimacy for government's embattled regulars surely is worth the effort. The Blacksburg Manifesto, which relies on constitutional legitimacy, resonates with a dignity deserved by dedicated public servants in the agencies. As the first coordinated effort to replace dysfunctional public administration orthodoxy, the manifesto blazed a path that subsequent efforts will gratefully follow, before they too face the undergrowth, but now using machetes whose edges have been spared the dulling effects of the first cut.

Ultimately constitutionalism fails us because it is simply too conservative; it is reactionary in the noble but still fettering Burkean sense. To defend the administrative state by constitutional inquiry looks back instead of forward. The attempt to save the administrative state from the attacks of primitive neoliberal philistines fights the battle on the wrong ground. One ends up forced to affirm many arrangements that merit, instead, reconstruction. Forced by the right-wing contras to a desperate redoubt, public administration theory finds itself fighting alongside such past and future nemeses as hierarchy, moribund institutional boundaries, agency aggrandizement (see, e.g., Kronenberg's 1990 challenge), and all the other bureau pathologies many of us had once hoped to surpass.

As the Blacksburg scholars admit (Wamsley et al. 1990, preface), they have come to embrace institutionalism and authority at least as a welcome alternative to the libertarian anarchy of the resurgent Right. We contend that this is overly defeatist. Defense of the status quo robs public administration theorists of the independence required to imagine more democratic and less constricting possibilities of work and governance. We should instead be alert to seize upon emerging trends and to coax from them a path toward a tolerant and nondogmatic administrative culture that respects contingency and surprise. Many niggling quarrels—such as the exclusion of dedicated state and local civil servants, the elitism implied by the role of the "upper reaches" of the civil service for which Rohr proposes a senatorial role—could (but won't) be picked. Other more substantive objections that we share with others (such as Stivers's [1993] charge of instrumentalism of the founders, or P. Cooper's [1990] demur relating to agencies' actual performance) need not be repeated here. Constitutionalism (and to the degree of reliance on same, the Blacksburg Manifesto[5]) ought not be afforded pride of place in the colloquy for an alternative model because it stoops to defensive and tortured argumentation; lacks a stable referent; and seems too closely tied, by virtue of the institutionalism implied, to a given structure of governance.

Tortured Argumentation

One cannot but admire the careful constitutional scholarship and the many hours of meticulous reading that Rohr (1986) exhibits in his *To Run a Constitution.* Few would agree to duel with him on these, his, grounds. He is also scrupulously honest about the results of these labors. The strongest case he can make for the constitutional legitimacy of public administration remains, by his admission, weak. Rohr would not ask for relaxed standards of judgment, or poetic license (174–78), were it not so. Because the cause—defending embattled bureaucrats—is just, we are asked to suspend normal protocols of scholarly argumentation. Aristotle's dictum that no more precision should be required than a subject admits is invoked to justify this suspension. At one point (176), novelty by itself stands as a criterion for positive evaluation of the argument. Even granting all such dispensations, in the end it is not so much that the Constitution founds public administration, as it is that public administration is not inconsistent with it. But by that logic, public administration is no less legitimate than, *tu quoque,* the imperial presidency, an activist judiciary, or, heaven forbid, the corps of Washington lobbyists. For such a diluted product, we think Rohr asks too dear a price. For violating the separation of powers, we are urged to adopt the most relaxed standards that can be read from Publius. For the independence to obey whichever master public administration deigns to hear, we are asked to acquiesce to the analogy of a long-since abandoned senatorial structure and its metaphoric balance wheel. The reasoning, although not exactly fallacious, nonetheless fails to persuade. An equally serious difficulty is what we call the riddle of the vanishing referent.

Vanishing Referent

The regime norms from which American bureaucrats are urged to deduce their ethics (Rohr 1989) are vanishing referents (Fox 1993). Like mirages and rainbows, they disappear when approached. So too seems the case with the cluster of concepts—*Constitution, principle, covenant, contract, tradition,* and *founding*—that Rohr uses to make his argument. In Rohr's text they are tautologically defined only in relation to each other. They take the form: What is X? It is Y. What is Y? It is Z. What is Z? It is X. (For example, what are constitutional values? They are regime values. What are regime values? They are the polity. What is the polity? That political entity that was brought into being by the ratification of the Constitution.) Like the classic caricature of a bureaucratic runaround, we are endlessly transferred to the next office without satisfaction. Specifically, if the Constitution owes its validity not to the document so named, but to a founding, and if the founding enacted a covenant that was itself based on the principles that bounded the argument, how can anything substantive about it be confidently asserted? Or indeed, with a little interpretive creativity, virtually anything could be audaciously asserted. If one is dissatisfied with the results of straightforward Constitution reading, just expand the parameters of the argument. How far from the framers and signers can we go? If we consult the antifederalists on the Left, as Rohr does, should we exclude British loyalists on the Right? If so, on what principle of exclusion? Should we not also consult (say) the recently unearthed diaries of the unindicted coconspirators of Shay's and the Whiskey rebellions? And what nominal time frame brackets the founding? Are we not still founding when we take the oath to uphold and support the argument? The point, overly made, is that constitutional legitimacy is a chimera wrapped in an enigma.

Communitarians would agree with us on that point. For them, it is the pursuit of the public interest and not a historical episode that legitimates the efforts of all who join with proactive public administrators, sometimes across institutional lines, in the endeavors of freedom and democracy.

Communitarian/Citizen Alternative

The other major contender to replace orthodoxy is citizen activation or civism. In public administration the legitimacy crisis is their entrée to the discourse caused by paradigm anxiety. As communitarianism is an essentially premodern philosophy, it has never been seen to illicitly associate with the utility-maximizing individualism that is presupposed by the loop model. The weakness of representative democracy represents, for communitarians, an opportunity to resuscitate the direct democracy of the community. Although the agencies that Blacksburg scholars would affirm may exhibit characteristics of community, their hierarchical structure and rigid turf-protectionist boundaries would surely be anathema to contemporary communitarians. Communitarians want strong democracy that leads to justice. People should be involved in the decisions that affect their lives, not only for the sake of justice, but also because the full development of their human potential requires it. People must involve themselves in the community to escape from the modern alienation that would otherwise typify their lives. The full development of human potential in community takes precedence over archaic constitutional debates and the current agential manifestations of these debates. Moreover, if the loop model is as dysfunctional as we have claimed, a logical alternative is to bypass the masters of ill-begotten political superordination and make common cause with the citizens themselves.

If the constitutional model harkens back to a sacred founding of the republic, citizen-administration solidarity harkens back to the direct democracy of the Athenian polis, the Swiss canton, and the New England town. Citizen engagement is both more diffusely defined than constitutionalism and possessed of a more complete standpoint (see Adams et al. 1990; Box 1998; Chandler 1984; T. L. Cooper 1991; Frederickson 1982; Gawthrop 1984; ; King and Stivers et al. 1998; Stivers 1990). It is a more thorough standpoint insofar as those advocating the citizen approach either implicitly or explicitly base their views on communitarianism. Communitarianism itself is a full-blown philosophical school strongly rooted in ancient (Aristotle), medieval (St. Thomas

Aquinas), and contemporary thought (e.g., Jonsen and Toulmin 1988; MacIntyre 1984; C. Taylor 1985; and to a lesser extent, Walzer 1983). Readers may be familiar with Bellah et al.'s (1985) *Habits of the Heart* and (1991) *The Good Society,* or Sandel's (1996) *Democracy's Discontent,* which are also rooted in communitarianism.

It might be helpful to briefly review the major tenets of philosophical communitarianism to see the power of it. Communitarianism can be portrayed in four steps. It has: (a) a different (from modernist liberal, classical liberal, or neoliberal) view of the self, which (b) alters the locus and direction of agential causality, which (c) calls forth a teleology of virtue or character ethics, which in turn (d) promotes a praxis typified by *phronesis* (practical wisdom). After we have reviewed these tenets we will point out the difficulties with this standpoint, note communitarian adjustments to account for these problems, and introduce the problem of citizen apathy, for which communitarians are insufficiently equipped.

Communitarianism: Bedrock View

The Self

The modern liberal understanding of the self supposes an atomistic (bourgeois) individual who rationally maximizes valuables unto its lonely self. Communitarians, on the other hand, worry about lifestyle agendas that lead to withdrawal from political engagement (Bennett 1998). Communitarians protest that the "self' presupposed in utilitarian doctrines is hardly a recognizable self at all. Such a cipher self has no culture, no history, and no situatedness; it is not embodied. It is an abstract self, a disembodied reasoning being theoretically fashioned after Descartes's cogito: "I think, therefore I am." Obversely, communitarianism follows Aristotle's dictum that a person is a social-political animal, the full development of which can only occur in a well-ordered community (polis). This more robust self comes stamped by its past community experience and does not have the absolute free will assumed for abstract, atomistic, and autonomous individuals.

The Primacy of Community

Communitarians begin not with the atomistic sovereign individual but with context. "They view human agency as situated in a concrete moral and political context and stress the constitutive role that communal aims and attachments assume for a situated self" (d'Entreves 1992, 180). Individuals, it follows, do not act as if in a vacuum. Causality—which in orthodox-liberal-modernist patterns runs from autonomous individual consciousness, to judgment or decision, to action—is now conceived by communitarians as a dialectical, reciprocal causality between individuals and the communal-historical context in which they have been formed. This context is already well populated with significant others. Indeed, without context the human individual is unimaginable—there would be no perceivable physiognomy, no temperament, no character, no flash of personality. An important implication of this shift in locus is to elevate the community to, if not absolute primacy, at least coequal causal primacy. In orthodoxy and neoliberalism, individual self-interest is assumed to be the primordial force in life, coordinated by the invisible hand of the market and tempered subsequently by an overlay of moral obligation dictated by right reason. In contrast, communitarians assume that the community itself and other humans are a precondition for human life and happiness. It follows that other-regardingness, altruism, loyalty, community attachments, and other group-based sentiments are not mere eccentric deviations from the norm of self-centered rationality, but are part of being in a human community. Attachments are not to be explained away as irrational exogenous factors but are there before the calculations of self-interest begin. This communitarian view undermines rational choice theory and dominant branches of economics (for public policy implications see Stone 1988).

Teleology of Virtue and Character

The cultivation of internal traits of character and virtue, then, is the goal of a well-ordered polis. Citizenship in a polis, by this view, is not simply a matter of convenient administration of affairs. Citizenship is a crucial part of the process of character cultivation. One does not emerge from the womb as a completely virtuous being nor does one suddenly become virtuous at puberty. Fully developed virtue and character, the telos of human life, require active participation in communal governance. The process of discourse with communal others, working out common ground, developing norms, is essential to the full development of human potential. Humans are political animals not only out of material need, but from their need for full spiritual maturation.

Phronesis

A well-ordered community of trust does not require rational-comprehensive social science. The latter, a mistake of the Enlightenment, assumes an impossible all-knowing God's-eye scan congruent only with predictable, rational, maximizing individuals. The looser but more realistic standards of *phronesis* (practical wisdom) are more suited to a discourse of communal citizens making decisions in concert. (See Flyvbjerg 2001 for a lengthy discussion of *phronesis* as a mode of social science research. See also D. F. Morgan 1990, for a discussion of *phronesis* specific to the problem of democratic public administration.) As Stivers (1990) has written: "The restoration of an understanding of governance as the exercise of practical wisdom . . . involves moving toward greater reliance on tentative strategies that self-correct through frequent feedback of information about their effects" (260).

Communitarianism: Criticisms and Responses

The Problems

Four overlapping problems quickly surface when one begins to think through communitarianism. If a major difficulty with orthodoxy and neoliberalism is the assumption of autonomous individualism, an abstraction of real situated individuals, the parallel problem with communitarianism is the assumption that communities are wholly or largely benign. Communitarianism has totalitarian tendencies, in that all aspects of life are gathered up, as it were, by the teleological thrust toward well-ordered harmony. At best, people may find this insufferably boring. At worst, eccentricities would be construed by community fussbudgets as inconsistent with community goals—mind-numbing conformity becomes the price of membership. The rights to privacy afforded sovereign individuals and the separate spheres (i.e., work, leisure, family, religion) carved out by liberal pluralism may be abrogated in communitarianism for the sake of community integrity, morality, or unity. Remember, too, for every misty dream of bucolic rural community there is an equally compelling vision of the dead weight of conformity enforced by community elders (elites) and self-appointed casuists. The dilemma may be instantly grasped by replacing the word *state* for *community* in all preceding sentences. A related problem is that communitarianism may be essentially an idealistic stained-glass-window nostalgia no longer viable as a real option in the mass societies inexorably created by advanced and postindustrial capitalism.

Adjustments to Base Communitarianism

The above difficulties of communitarianism have not gone unnoticed by its public administration champions. T. L. Cooper (1987, 1991) has tried to accommodate them by amendment. Acknowledging the incorrigible actuality of pluralism, Cooper avoids the nostalgia and totalitarian traps mentioned above. Adopting Cochran's (1982) innovative theoretical move, he conceptualizes community in pluralistic, associational terms, hence freeing community from the confinement of geographical jurisdiction. Thus rendered, community becomes more like an electronically augmented, communication-age affinity group. This allows communities with qualities similar to Tocqueville's voluntary associations to serve as mediating institutions between (merely) legal citizens and government. By *legal citizens* Cooper means minimalist citizenship consistent with atomistic passive individuals possessing the usual rights and freedoms—what Berlin (1979) aptly calls negative freedom. Within these associations lies the potential for communities. The communitarian milieu, where full ethical citizenship flourishes, is nurtured in these communities.

The citizen-administrator encourages these communities and dialectically intermingles with them. Administrators themselves are ethically nourished and cocreated within professional communities in government (Stivers 1990, 267ff. makes a similar point). This sort of professionalism is distinguished from the sort of professionalism entailed by guild protectionism. That sort of professionalism has been criticized as a conspiracy against the laity, a self-serving professionalism illegitimately cooked up behind veils of expertise, technique, and credentialing. MacIntyre's (1984) distinction between internal and external goods of a practice is appropriated for the purpose of distinguishing between ethical professionalism and self-serving professionalism (T. L. Cooper 1987). Professionalism must remain open to external influences. This theoretical move creates a complex array of overlapping communities synergistically cocreating ethical citizens, some of whom also will be ethical citizen-administrators. As in Barber's (1984, 2004) strong democracy, not only would such a scheme provide for will formation and legitimate governance, but—more important to communitarians—it would also encourage the full development of human potential, which fulfills the teleological obligation to participate in community decisions that affect both the individual and the commonweal (Cochran 1982, cited in T. L. Cooper 1991, 160). We will adopt many of these amendments and co-opt them as integral parts of discourse theory. Other adjustments cannot be abided.

Both Cooper and Stivers have anticipated a response to a class of objections that idealism of any sort is liable to attract. What is the response to the criticism that the existing society and existing culture obviate deployment of the communitarian model? The answer is the "tension between the real and ideal" gambit. Stivers (1990) has gone so far as to turn the lack of correspondence between real and ideal into a virtue: "Unless we understand that our intentions—the ends for which the state was formed—are out of reach, we will be unable to practice the trust in one another that enables us to accept the inevitable imperfections of actual policies" (254).

We can only point out that such a gambit can be used on behalf of any ideal. If we are going to imagine ideals validated by the distance of them from the existent, why not imagine one where the state has withered away, humans have transcended scarcity, labor is no longer forced by survival needs, and administration is over only things, not people? Why not dream beyond Marx of the *German Ideology* and the *Grundrisse* instead of dreaming only beyond Skinner of *Walden II?*

On the matter of citizen apathy, the communitarian ideal is especially problematic.

The Problem of Citizen Apathy

Communitarianism, we believe, stumbles over the problem of citizen apathy. Communitarians cannot abide indifference and inattention among the would-be citizenry. We, on the other hand, believe the apathetic have a right to their ways.

If most people are not much interested in matters of governance, the communitarian model would seem an unlikely proposition. Teenagers capable of infinitely varied and precise recognition of categories of sports shoes, trousers, and other fashions cannot name cabinet-level agencies. But before the hand wringing begins, a pause may be in order. Perhaps we are the arrogant ones, we professional political junkies, policy wonks, and government watchers. Imagine the range of human endeavor that we also neglect. Our close attention to issues of governance should not lead us to assume that others would be equally attentive if left to their own devices. Perhaps the communitarian fulfillment by the governmentally apathetic could come not from governing in the usual sense of self-government, but from participation in all the other myriad forms of self-through-community actualization available to them, including car racing, dog clubs, RV clubs, church activities, little leagues, fan clubs, gangs, and Bible reading groups. The comforting knowledge that one could at any time *become* active and have influence seems enough democracy for the average middle-class citizen.

Furthermore, it is easy to make the *standpunkt* error of falsely conflating community governance with what our public administrationists' perspective has labeled governance. We have reified the term *governance,* confusing the given conception with the thing itself. Indeed, the usual and immediately apparent reaction to the juxtaposition of some form of ideal democracy, on the one hand, with evidence of citizen apathy, on the other, is to assume that apathy is unnatural and has been caused by some fundamental flaw in the political or societal structure. Further, we should strive to overcome this flaw, this apathy. This response is doubly seductive from the communitarian perspective, where participation is a necessary component of being human at all. To leave people alone with their apathy is to consign them to the status of *untermenschen.* If we do not wish to "force them to be free," would it be all right if we merely empower them (Adams et al. 1990)? Empowerment would bring into the community those citizens who have been shut out. Certain reforms flow from this view. Voter registration regulations should be reformed to make it easier to vote; policy analysis should avoid jargon so that normal citizens can understand the issues; sunshine legislation should be pursued to ensure that citizens have adequate access to information; public-interest TV channels should be set up to counter the tendency for media to be monopolized or oligopolized in fewer and fewer hands. The theory of empowerment is behind the laudable efforts described in *Government Is Us* (King and Stivers et al. 1998). We urge strong and active support for all such measures, but it is our skeptical guess that they will not be able to significantly counterbalance the inertia of citizen inattention. Sunshine legislation and open hearings only made budgetary markup sessions more accessible to well-heeled and well-organized special interest groups, not to the citizenry at large. Giving citizens the theoretical capability of obtaining more information on top of the information they already ignore is not helpful to them. It is, however, helpful to the attentive citizens, those who engage their intellect, passion, and personal reputations with the issues.

In a community where the general citizenry is inattentive except during crises or when malfeasance has become egregious, democracy may be *for* the people but it cannot be claimed that it is *of* or *by* the people. Mass democracy exists only as potential—a potential that should, of course, be preserved at all costs. For the remainder, we have a discourse of "citizens in lieu of the rest of us" (Walzer 1970, 216).

Community Over All

This next sort of problem is glossed over by communitarians who, to their credit we believe, argue for a stronger sense of *res publica* (the public thing), but lack a good line of demarcation as to where the public thing should cease. Put another way, we would like to retain a measure of classical libertarian tolerance for those who step outside of the dominant social and moral codes. But Bellah et al. (1991) argue for a democratic society that contains, among other things, a "public church." They are not intending to prescribe a state religion or a governmental church, but, "in two senses," the authors of *The Good Society* write, "religion cannot be private."

> Firstly, both Christians and Jews recognize a God who created heaven and earth, all that is, seen and unseen, whose dominion clearly transcends not only private life but the nations themselves. There is nothing in the private or public realm that cannot concern such a religious tradition. Secondly "public" came to mean the citizenry who reflect on matters of common concern, engage in deliberation together, and choose their representatives to constitute the government, whose powers are limited by a constitution. Religious bodies are very much part of *this* meaning of the public . . . because they enter into the common discussion about the public good. (Bellah et al. 1991, 179)

Bellah and his associates presume "religious bodies" are able to speak in the common discussion, a presumption that calls forth a series of problems lurking just beneath the surface of community.

Intrusive Fussbudgets

In the quotation above, Bellah et al. assert that "There is nothing in the private or public realm that cannot concern such a religious tradition."

Now if one is neither a Christian nor a Jew, the notion that Christians and Jews would declare the public at large (or "nations themselves") to be their domain is not necessarily reassuring. Indeed, with nothing off-limits to community strictures that are not one's own, one might be worried that one's opportunities to live life as one wishes in a non-Christian or non-Jewish manner would diminish. Private space is particularly vulnerable to communitarian encroachments.

The more things called sin, the more sin. There are some places where public administrators ought not tread, or at least ought to tread lightly, justly, rarely, and solicitously. We are unable to specify the line where off-limits issues begin; but surely not all issues are public issues. The claims of pursed-lipped fussbudgets enforcing the lesser mandates of the community do not always trump the claims of the individual of classical liberalism. The association here is that the total-inclusion model of communitarianism, as espoused by Bellah et al. (1991), is coercively so. Good intentions notwithstanding, that sort of homogeneous community looks identical to a totalitarian state.

Spicer (2001) claims that any proposal entailing harmony of human purposes now lacks credibility. The communitarian thrust in public administration may simply be inappropriate. "[I]t becomes increasingly likely that acts of public administrators, when directed toward the achievement of particular substantive purposes and values, will inevitably come to be seen as repressive by those who do not share these purposes and values" (101). Spicer (2003, following Berlin 1969) distinguished between negative freedom and positive freedom. Negative freedom is about leaving people alone so long as they are not interfering with anyone. Positive freedom is a more proactive version of freedom, entailing the development of human potential through the use of political power. Communitarians, it seems to us, have downplayed negative freedom in their enthusiasm for positive freedom. Negative freedom is more than a defense of laissez-faire individualism; it is an indispensable part of the language against totalitarianism.

So far, then, we have noted several tendencies against public administration orthodoxy. We have noted that neoliberal managerialism tries and to some extent succeeds in deregulating the bureaucracy, and also functions to limit and in some cases dismantle government as well. Otherwise, neoliberalism preserves or extends status quo power relations. Despite the market rhetoric of neoliberal reform, the norms of orthodoxy—efficiency, rationality, and the legitimacy of the loop model of democracy

—retain their status. Nor were we entirely pleased with the conservatism of the constitutionalist alternative, and thought its referencing a vanishing founding to be frustrating. Finally, we thought civism to be an unlikely solution amidst an apathetic citizenry despite the strengths of its communitarian underpinnings. The potential for a smothering conformity to group norms also gave us pause, despite its concurrent and welcome retreat from orthodox individualism.

In the next chapter we contemplate a new problematic that complicates and makes more difficult any alternative reform proposal: *hyperreality.*

Notes

1. We would like to thank Michael Spicer for informing this discussion.

2. This is not the place to gather up all critiques of orthodoxy. Hierarchy and scientific management have been savaged by vast literatures, ranging from efficiency orientations of organization theory to the ambient health of the collective unconscious of Jungian psychology. We are also bypassing the literature on bureaucrat bashing to avoid casting the discretionist school as an ill-tempered reaction formation.

3. Rohr (1993) is certainly right to complain in a *PAR* symposium on this matter that Spicer and Terry have misread him. It is not the character of the particular founders that is at issue. They are but a conduit to a higher Truth. He is, as they are, looking for a certain underlying, or rather, superordinate calculus. This calculus is not the logic of formalized self-interest à la Buchanan and Tullock (1962), but the *telos* of a *polis*; the appropriate arrangements for the development of virtue.

4. Although this interpretation is well grounded in Rohr's texts, we must confess to a little exegesis ourselves. This is an unauthorized interpretation.

5. Despite their professed reliance on constitutionalism, much of the manifesto could be salvaged if they would abandon it. Goodsell's case for the public interest, that part of the agency perspective that is not wedded to institutions as given, and White's discourse on authority not only can stand alone, but, in our opinion, would be improved if they did (both essays in Wamsley et al. 1990).

3

Hyperreality

Instability and Incommensurability

As orthodoxy would have it, the sovereign people express their will through the democratic accountability feedback loop, which is elaborated in rules and enforced through the chain of command. If the critique of that model were not enough to justify the need for a new normative theory of democratic possibilities in the United States, we now want to augment the critique with an explication of hyperreality. The effects of this chapter, if valid, will render more implausible (1) loop strategies of reviving overhead democracy, (2) neoliberal reforms aimed at making government run like a business, (3) constitutionalist schemes of grounding agency in the founding, and (4) communitarian solutions based on citizen involvement. This chapter deals with the public conversation, which has become problematic for democracy.

The rapidity and velocity of information flow, which is to say symbolic communication, has changed the nature of communication. It is not only that "the media is the message" as Marshall MacLuhan noted, but that mass communication, information exchange, and diffusion of symbolic expression has increased in speed and velocity. The increasingly predominant hyperreality of signs influenced by TV, the Internet, cell phones, iPods, and other forms of communication devices has changed things in ways that modern conceptualizations do not quite capture. Hyperreality is left largely unexamined or (in our view) underemphasized in the modern canon. Our analysis is influenced by the postmodern politics of signs.

America today shares across disparate groups and tribes only a media-infused hyperreality of consciousness. This reality is transient and unstable and mutates rapidly. It is, as we will try to demonstrate, thin.

Concomitantly, second, there is a refracted, more intimate, but perhaps incommensurable series of realities constructed by multiple subcultural fragments (Calinescu 1991; Jameson 1991). The state, will formation, problem solving, managerialism, outcomes measurement, citizen participation, and constitutional foundationalism are all problematic in hyperreality. The term *hyperreality* is used here to gather in the tendencies we just mentioned, most especially: (a) the transient, unstable, rapidly mutating media-infused reality; and (b) incommensurable realities distributed among diverse subcultural groups. Our journey through hyperreality can be divided into five legs:

1. Signs, the symbols through which the public conversation is communicated, have become self-referential and epiphenomenal (i.e., derivative or second order).
2. The accompanying danger is that diverse subcultures talk past one another (i.e., language games are incommensurable).
3. The political implications of hyperreality—a rapid sequence of images and symbols with unknown or uncertain referents racing through the public consciousness—are that simulation and media spectacle displace political debate.
4. The continuous struggle for meaning capture implies that symbolic politics, largely divorced from material distribution of valuables, matters most.
5. The effects of hyperreality on orthodoxy and its neoliberal, constitutionalist and communitarian competitors require assessment.

The next three sections explore hyperreality. We adduce evidence of, and the political prospects of, a world without anchor, cultures without stable referents, and decentered selves without identities from which to speak or gesture.

Unstable Signs Leading to a Virtual Reality

The important effect of hyperreality, from the vantage point of political science and public administration, is that it hobbles government and renders dubious national policymaking in any sense of national interest. The contemporary era is in danger of developing a politics of simulation or virtual reality, useful as a spectacle or entertaining diversion but not much help with the problems of governance. The postmodern voice provides the clearest possible rendering of what we mean by simulated politics.

Stable Communication/Epiphenomenalism

The point we want to make in this section is that words, signs, and symbols have become increasingly divorced from what in modernity was taken for reality-as-such, a real reality and not some socially constructed reality. This is what we mean by *epiphenomenalism.* Words, signs, and symbols are increasingly unlikely to mean anything solid or lasting. Postmodern theory gives interpretive depth to these nonreferential aspects of language. We are rendered speechless by such tendencies as media-induced consumerism, negative political advertisements, sound-bite and photo-op political journalism, and media-assisted forms of deception. In order to assess the radical epiphenomenalism of signs, a base by which their distance from referents may be so judged is required.

This section is not offered as a careful argument of semiotics or epistemology, but rather is similar in purpose to Baudrillard's (1983, 11 ff.) speculations or Jameson's (1991 96) use of the *imaginary* to express a similar point. Sustained rigorous arguments that are compatible include Habermas (1972, especially chapter 5), Wittgenstein (1953), and Baudrillard (1981, 158 ff.), on whom we shall rely for insights into epiphenomenal hyperreality.

Subsection 1, on denotation/connotation, contemplates some problems in ascribing the prestige of denotation to social science phenomena. Subsection 2, on the human tendency toward abstraction, explores the stability of modernist metanarratives, against which hyperreality seems spectral and haunting. Subsection 3, on production/information, offers both political-economic evolutions and philosophical turns as being influential in the thinning of reality.

Denotation/Connotation

Language in modernity was anchored by direct one-to-one picture representations of objects. Although this view lives on in the unexamined assumptions of sophomoric science, it is no longer hegemonic in philosophy or semiotics. Wittgenstein (1953) has taught us that strictly denotative signs are not the paradigmatic cornerstone of communication. Denotative signs have, when uttered, already connotative implications, which depend on the context in which they are used. Hence, a good starting point in recognizing the difficulty of symbolic communication is the denotation-connotation difference.

Denotation is usually taken to mean a straightforward signifier. Red traffic signal means stop. Connotation, on the other hand, implicates an extension of meaning apart from the explicit thing being named. Red may mean roses, or passion, or blood, or wine, or prostitution, or socialism, or magnanimity. Against denotation, Barthes (1977) predicted that, "the future probably belongs to a linguistics of connotation" (90). The reason is that connotation implies diffusion. It is the more general concept, but it never totally overtakes denotation.

Writing before the age of digital photography, Barthes (1978) conceived of the photographic image as a denotative one (or so it seems years later): "What does the photograph transmit? By definition, the scene itself, the literal reality . . . . Certainly the image is not the reality but at least it is its perfect *analogon* and it is exactly this analogical perfection which, to common sense, defines the photograph" (16). Of course, Barthes did not naïvely hold this view of the denotative photograph—he appreciated that trick effects, posing, and other ways of staging a photograph allowed the photographer to benefit from the prestige of denotation while performing a connotative act. The point is that even the quintessentially denotative photograph can be connotative— a structured signification that codes and communicates something quite different from reality-in-itself.

The photograph, like other forms of cultural expression, possesses connotative characteristics and does not merely re-present reality. Derrida has struggled mightily to assign linguistics (writing in particular) a responsibility and a status that extends beyond the denotative. One could (and most of us typically do) habitually think of "reality" as the imitated and "art" (or any representational symbol) as the imitator. This is the style of thinking of those who are committed to Truth. The phrase "Life imitates art" is a sort of joke. In postmodern thought it seems closer to a truism. Derrida sides with art, or more specifically with writing, rather than Truth. He complains about the tradition in which writing is subordinated to "a truth adequately represented" (1991, 181). What about those instances when the imitator has no imitated, the signifier no signified, the sign no referent? What about those Internet moments when the message has no speaker? These instances are not digestible in reality-system thinking. Derrida (1991) annihilates denotation this way:

"The operation, which no longer belongs to the system of truth, does not manifest, produce, or unveil any presence; nor does it constitute any conformity, resemblance, or adequation between a presence and a representation" (191–92). Less abstrusely, one could say that the connotative gathers up the denotative and provides the purposeful reason for its deployment.

Abstraction

The ability of humans to use signs under modalities of cooperation carries with it the transcendent talent of abstraction and use of metaphors. Humans also enjoy using startling oppositions, provoking laughter. With a memory capable of mixed scanning and categorical sorting, along with the playful capacity to exaggerate, mimic, lie, and act out (dogs, for instance, cannot feign excitement) the human talent for communication leads not only to storytelling, but also to theory, philosophy, and religion. These cultural creations are manifested in reification and hypostatization (construing a conceptual entity as a real existent). The abstraction, be it a category, a story, or an entire religion, is objectified or "thingified"; a hegemonic reality is attributed to it.

The history of civilization is filled with incidents of abstract thought racing beyond everyday life to confuse and overwhelm its denotative-connotative gestures. Religious wars may be counted among the instances where abstractions ascend over the discourse of everyday contingency. Although abstract thought of any kind may be regarded as just that—abstract and with problematic relation to the denotative-connotative continuum—abstractions may also be categorized as having more or less density and fixity. We are leading up to the claim that reifications circulating in hyperreality have less of such density and fixity.

Production/Information

As long as most humans were forced to earn their living by producing commodities in groups, a sufficiently robust linguistic base of denotative-connotative communicative speech acts would refer to the real commodities planted and harvested, crafted, or rolled off the assembly line. And accurate, robust communication would be required for the cooperative acts needed to produce them. In the realm of civil society, relatively stable family units, neighborhoods, and religious communities would also assure sufficient human interaction to provide a bedrock of grounded communication. The thesis of Jean Baudrillard (1981, chapter 2)—corresponding to insights from sociologists such as Daniel Bell, communication theorists such as Marshall McLuhan, and neo-Marxist political economy (see Kellner 1989; Poster 1990)—is that this robust base is lost when advanced industrial societies move from an emphasis on production to an emphasis on consumption and information. As fewer and fewer people earned their living by growing, mining, and manufacturing commodities, as machines and electrification replaced brute human labor, and now as more and more people earn their vouchers to consume by manipulating information and symbols (often persuading others to consume), the viscosity of reality thins. This thinning is exacerbated by the exponential multiplication of advertising messages that inundate consumers, informing them that consumption is now vastly more important than production.[1] There is, we think, a direct connection between postindustrial society and hyperreality.

The concomitant thinning of superstructural metanarratives has been the main work of philosophy in the last half of the twentieth century. As Rome was battered and finally destroyed by successive waves of barbarians, so has the foundationalist/modern metanarrative canon been battered by Nietzsche, pragmatists, existentialists, phenomenologists, semioticians, poststructuralists, deconstructionists, hermeneuticists, and more. All the metanarratives of science, metaphysics, and epistemology are being mercilessly deconstructed with the same tools used against premodern defenses of religion. Reason and science, having triumphed over supernaturalism and superstition, have turned back on themselves and have eroded their own bases of confident assertion.

Referents Yield to Self-Referential Signs

The change from a production economy to an economy centered on consumption provides the historical conditions for this postindustrial hyperreality. Denotative signs occurred within stable language games of modernity where truth seemed an observable or at least denotable matter. Epiphenomenal signs rely more on each other (i.e., they are *self-referential*). Unmoored with respect to any foundation, they begin to float away from any foundational truths (making them epiphenomenal).

Baudrillard (1983) goes so far as to claim that nonreferential signs take charge (sort of a semiotic hegemony) and determine the real.

Jameson (1991) has called this the "free and random play of signifiers" (96). But the dynamic pattern by which signs become self-referential is another matter. The following moments of our thesis each require explication:

1. The spread of monologic communication,
2. Leading to the creation of pseudocommunities, and
3. Allowing the free-play of signifiers to become self-referential.

Monologic Communication

If one accepts the proposition that reality is a social construction or structuration (this topic will be taken up in chapter 4) it follows that intersubjective interaction and communication generate this social construction of reality. An intersubjective reality would have a certain quality stemming from the heterogeneity of those whose acts, words, and gazes that hold the community together. Active participants sustain their reality via a denotative-connotative language game where there is a verbal struggle over both the denotation and the connotation of signs. This is how reality is negotiated, created, and constituted.

However, that kind of intersubjective social communication is disrupted in hyperreality, and the roots of the disruption may be traced to modernist practices. Hummel (1994) identifies a monologic form of communication and links it to bureaucratized language, in which the world of robust social action is displaced by the world of rationally organized, bureaucratic action. Obedience to hierarchically commanded routines supersedes empathic relationships with clients; savvy clients who regularly interact with functionaries learn to separate meaning from the message. And in bureaucracy, because language is separated from the intentions of the speaker, the individual functionary need not be personally committed to his or her words. To blame the functionary for official utterances is to mistake one-dimensional monologue for robust social conversation. One does not have normal social conversations with bureaucratized functionaries; problem solving or social sense making will not occur—the problem has been preidentified and its solution already put into place (Hummel 1994). There is no dialogue, no opportunity to express a different conceptualization, no opportunity to engage in a verbal struggle to define a problem and decide what should be done about it.

Instead of *communal* or *dialogic* communication, the dominant mode of message transfer is *monologic*. The first moment of this transformation is the separation of the role of speaker/listener into two roles. The next moment begins with the increasing ubiquity and hegemony of one-way utterances, unchecked by the possibility of immediate retort. Hence the communal dialogue devolves into a monologue.

Another paradigm case is the rise and spread of broadcast media. The deduction that broadcast media are monologic requires little demonstration. Obviously, most viewers and listeners cannot talk back. Neither talk shows nor "interactive" TV indicates an exception to the general monologue. There is virtually no communicative reciprocity, no dialogue; one can only switch channels or turn off the set. On behalf of "broadcast central," affirmation is measured in Nielsen-type ratings, market share, and the viewer's subsequent purchase of advertised products. But even here an atomistic individual is only marginally empowered to affirm or negate. What an individual personally watches or turns off is unlikely to be charted; an n of 1 makes no significant ripple on the statistical charts. The monologue needs the participation of no one in particular. Response is diffuse.

Pseudocommunities

Monologic community alters radically the notion of community. The term *broadcast*, for example, implies casting from some central location to an unspecified, dispersed audience of receivers. An epiphenomenal message sent from a central location can be received by millions of viewers and auditors. The sound bite and image go forth to create a chaotic, constantly shifting pseudocommunity momentarily brought together only by that message. This pseudocommunity need not share class position, worksite, age, gender, geographic area, or ideological predisposition. The pseudocommunity changes actual membership each nanosecond, even while being constant in a statistical sense.

At the receiving end of the encoding-decoding communication sequence are vastly varied levels of attention and engagement—from the passive, dazed, half-drunk couch potato to the channel-surfing stimulation glutton (expressing two responses to boredom). The participation that does occur is very much controlled and allowed only on terms set by broadcast central: send money to the televangelist to continue the mission; see your pledge registered on the big board; call in to *Larry*

King Live; compete for a place on the game show; vacation in Holly-wood and be part of a "live" audience; display your talents (or lack thereof) on national TV before a panel of judges; become a participant in "reality TV."

Self-Referencing

Without situated and contextualized community, TV communication is more or less self-contained and is thus self-referential. On TV, history is a rerun of the black-and-white TV programs shown during the Kennedy administration, or a thirty-second spot about the "historic Ice Bowl" football game. The more a language or practice is removed from con-text, where social relationships would be reproduced through dialogue, the more language must mimic those features from within itself. Media-generated epiphenomenal language must simulate its context and ven-triloquize its audience.

Because there is no clearly determinate referential world outside the broad-cast to provide a standard against which to evaluate the flow of meanings, subjects have no defined identity as players in the conversation. When that is the case (i.e., no constraining resistance of an alternatively constitutive ontological base), the real is only self-referentially so (Poster 1990, 45).

Programming may be seen as self-referential in the sense of comply-ing with a master template etched by the imperatives of clock time. The length of programming and consequently its level of generalization are not, like primordial language games or even books, substantively driven. They are arranged according to clock time to regularize the audience and to accommodate the selling of commercial slots. The amount of time to be filled is given and determining. The plots of sitcoms or detec-tive cop shows are driven by the rhythm of commercial breaks and con-flict resolution on the half-hour or hour. Miniscule changes in diffuse audience preferences doom one series while vaulting to fame the virtu-ally interchangeable stars of other almost-identical ones.

But it is in news broadcasting—putatively the reflection of the real upon which public policy might be based—that self-referential hyperreality is most apparent. The distinction between news and enter-tainment is increasingly permeable (e.g., Arnold Schwarzenegger became governor of California; *The Today Show* is a news-entertainment-educational-commercial promo mélange). *Al Jazeera* notwithstanding, Americans do not get different news from different networks. From an almost infinite number of potential events that could become news, virtually the same events will be reported in the twenty-two minutes allowed by each network for the news. News is not so much what happens as what gets reported. In this sense the news is created by the media from ambient events and happenings. Once an event or persona has been thus vaulted to the realm of media happening, he, she, or it is vested with newsworthiness and becomes part of hyperreality. Once part of hyperreality, they are analyzed by talking heads, become metaphors to shape perception of other events, are reprised at year-end as one of the top ten stories, and are historicized by recall at every anniversary divisible by ten.

Again, as hyperreality has no anchor in dialogic discourse, no check outside itself, the dynamic of it favors increasing shrillness, vulgarity, shock-value depictions of violence, bizarre human relationships and ever more provocative and insulting talk show hosts. From the moment one gets up at the urging of the clock radio, through breakfast with Katie and Matt, and then traffic updates and happy talk during long commutes, to prime-time TV at night, one is inundated by messages. Naturally, broadcasters are motivated to shrillness to ensure that their voices pierce through what one might otherwise take as part of background white noise. This hyperreality would disintegrate under norms of democratic deliberation, where challenges could be offered and claims could be judged against agreed-upon standards.

The Thinning of Reality

The first section of this chapter established modernity as a ground of relatively stable communication and then ascertained the historical conditions of its erosion, setting the stage for the epiphenomenal signifiers. The second section explicated a pattern (exemplified by broadcast media) whereby signs become self-referential. We now turn to the question: How pervasive is the thinning of "reality"? Or, less ambitiously, what other signatures of self-referential signs may be adduced? Let's take an airplane trip, go to a theme park, and experience a war.

Monological Communication in Serialized Communities

As we have argued, modernity possessed shared standards from which truth functions could be derived. Modernity had totalitarian tendencies, but we could in common assess the truth of such claims as "the trains run on time." We knew what trains were, we had timetables to tell us what "on time" meant, and we had clocks that reported time. Now the claim that planes run on time can be assessed only by a statistical artifact developed by airlines to prove that they do. Worse, this statistical artifact is believably delivered to us by our surrogate sister or brother, the flight attendant, in ways that invite neither questioning nor dissent. Likewise, passengers herded and cramped into a stuffy, crowded plane parked on the tarmac are thanked for the patience they neither felt nor expressed. Dialogue and information dissemination are possible, but passengers are instead treated like media consumers and their response is ventriloquized. Passengers, perhaps conditioned to silent acquiescence to what is broadcast, do not demand the precise meaning of "short delay." Announcements are monologic. Passengers, as undifferentiated ciphers, are a pseudocommunity thrown together by random forces. They are what Sartre (Hirsh 1981, 76ff.) would call a serialized group, a series of otherwise atomized individuals brought together only by the coincidence of an airplane schedule. Atomized, they have none of the solidarity of community, through which they might demand better treatment and more human mutuality.

Vacations, too, are spent consuming monologues in serialized pseudocommunities, especially at theme parks. Long queues are artfully designed to give the appearance of progress toward the attraction; young interchangeable guides spiel humorous patois by rote to acquiescent individuals and families thrown together by chance. Photos of the simulated good time, suitable for framing, may be purchased at the conclusion. If not, helpful signs erected by Kodak (a logo) will tell one where to snap to preserve the memory of what never was. And, wherever one goes, one arrives at a destination in which the milieu is almost the same as the one just left: same airport, same restaurants, same freeways leading to the same mall. Populating these facade simulacra are interchangeable people, ciphers with the corporate uniform, logo, and smile. The many actors fitting themselves into Mickey Mouse suits in Disney theme parks in California, Florida, Tokyo, and France become simulacra of an imaginary mouse. History itself becomes commoditized simulacra: Colonial Williamsburg with its (oxymoronic) "authentic reproductions"; the movie set for the epic film *Alamo* (more popular than the real [i.e., authentically reproduced] one). And coming soon for your enjoyment is interactive virtual reality from within a wireless headset.

Can the Real Be Distinguished from the Virtual?

Can humans sustain the modern ability to differentiate between hyperreality on the one hand, and reality on the other? Or have reality-in-itself and reality (the symbol for same) merged at the point where reality morphs into hyperreality? After all, even war seems epiphenomenal, like a TV miniseries followed by talk show discussions and then parades. But a TV miniseries would seem more real than the way the Gulf War has been experienced. In the first Gulf War, viewers saw journalists breathlessly groping for their gas masks, ambiguous pictures of greenish fireworks incoherently interpreted by the reporters on the scene. Then "public information" officers (journalists in uniform) briefed civilian journalists; and then journalists interviewed retired military experts (now employed as journalists); then journalists talked to other journalists about the plight of journalists in hotels (Bernie was under the table, suicidal Peter (who would be fired by CNN at the onset of the second Gulf War) was looking out the window). Then journalists analyzed the role of journalism in modern warfare. But this analysis did not prevent them from being "embedded" with the troops in the next Gulf War to eat, live, and die with them. The message is the self-referential media.

The news reporters become the news. Judith Miller, the *New York Times* reporter who went to jail to protect her confidential sources is a case in point. While adherence to this protect-your-sources principle would normally count as a form of journalistic martyrdom, it turned out that the source she was protecting was I. Lewis Libby, a White House spin fabricator. Before Libby's indictment, Miller herself had become the news because of her jail time. But before she became the news, she had become notorious for repeating misinformation from the White House, published in the *New York Times,* about the presence of weapons of mass destruction in Saddam Hussein's Iraq—which was the Bush administration's rationale for going to war. It turns out not to have been a "rationale" in the sense of a coherent argument backed by evidence, despite its success in keeping war funding on track.

Neotribalism and the Decentered Self

At a level of abstraction worthy of Hegel, Spengler, and Toynbee, the demise of a hegemonic entity results in centripetal fragmentation. When what is perceived in common across classes, genders, and regions as reality turns out to be self-referential; vacuous, diverse worldviews of previously oppressed subcultures gain relative respect. Some of these worldviews, shaped by peculiarities of cultural practices and beliefs, are already complete, and are now freed to express their holographic visions and particular interpretations unimpeded by the resistance heretofore afforded by a universalistic hegemonic worldview. At the macrolevel reality is thin. At microlevels, thick interpretations of "reality" fill the legitimacy vacuum. Queer nation, religious denominations, various jihadists, branch Davidians, black nationalists, Aryan nation, crips, and other groups sally forth with self-referencing paradigms that members can be taught. Put another way, the thinness of the putatively dominant, shared culture calls forth a plurality of thick, robust, self-contained communities, the borders of which are watchfully guarded by their leaders and intellectuals.

The crucial question is whether this plurality of views is a new tribalism, prelude to a tower of Babel, or a precondition for an enriched discourse freed from the fetters of the monolithic modern canon. The cogency of the contrary tribalism thesis we present next rests on three interrelated themes of postmodern thought: (1) otherness and difference, (2) incommensurability between others, and (3) the decentered self.

Otherness and Incommensurability

The legitimization of "otherness" and "difference" follows from the demise of modern foundationalism and incredulity toward its metanarratives. Again, the demise of universal metanarratives puts previously stable meanings in play; they are up for grabs. Feminists and other groups of others, those who embody difference, claim quite reasonably that the now-discredited universality of the canons of the Enlightenment were but the special pleadings of white, propertied, patriarchal, Eurocentric privileged classes. Other, different ways of being and ways of seeing merit heightened respect because of past suppression by those (what we now know as) partial but canonically arrogant worldviews. Moreover, other, different ways of being and ways of seeing merit extra consideration because of past suppression under the influence of the dominant metanarrative (now viewed as illegitimately dominant). Hence Zurab Tsereteli's 311–foot statue of the great sea captain Christopher Columbus, intended as a goodwill

gift from Russia on the 500th anniversary of his voyage to San Salvador, goes begging for a home, its head in Fort Lauderdale and the
other pieces, last we heard, still in St. Petersburg, Russia. "Others"
have judged Columbus guilty of genocide and exploitation and are
unwilling any longer to be victims of the hegemony in which they
are otherized.

But here is a problem. If all pleadings are special, why would any
individual situated in one subcultural fragment with its particular
worldview bother to assess the validity of different ones? If one's otherness and difference are to be celebrated, it follows that precisely
those aspects of an identity that are radically other would be accentu-
ated while similarities would be minimized or ignored. The proliferation of othernesses means that social fragmentation persists and
distends.

The plurality of thick paradigms of subcultures, enabled by the
depthlessness of common culture and illegitimacy of high culture, raises
the specter of incommensurability (see Bernstein 1992, chapter 3, for
accessible explication). Attention to the problem of incommensurability,
as a matter of intellectual history, has been largely the result of Kuhn's
(1970) best seller, *The Structure of Scientific Revolutions.* Kuhn argued that scientific paradigms are, in relation to one another, incommensurable. A paradigm is a system of logically interrelated
propositions, the sum of which is taken to adequately explain phenomena in a given field of scientific inquiry. Paradigms become threatened when phenomena do not behave according to a paradigm's
propositions; these phenomena are called anomalies. The proliferation of anomalous phenomena gives rise to competing theoretical systems that claim to better account for all phenomena previously
explained, as well as the anomalies that have emerged. Science
progresses, according to Kuhn, by the revolutionary vanquishing of an
older paradigm by a newer one. Kuhn's history of science, however,
indicated that the victory of one paradigm over another is less a matter
of superior coherence and explanatory fecundity and more a matter of
the displacement of the old paradigm by a newer one. Discussion, dialogue, and academic disputation do not settle the anomalies because
radically different presuppositions are not amenable to evidence or
refutation; the presuppositions determine in advance what evidence is
acceptable as refutation. One set of paradigmatic assumptions simply
cannot "see" evidence and data thrown up by a different set.

Fractions and Fragments

If people talk past one another in science, the bastion of reason and exemplar of civil disputation, can we expect better from other cults? If science operates by way of decidedly uncivil paradigmatic revolutions, can we expect better modes of conflict resolution between, say, right-wing skinheads and urban gangs? Can civility and trans-paradigmatic empathy be expected between those who believe they are victimized by Eurocentric cultural dominance and those whose life project has been precisely dedicated to the preservation and dissemination of Shakespeare, Milton, Plato, and the traditions which such figures express? Does one group have to die of old age to allow the fruition of otherness? Kuhn's work with hard science, where evidence might be more compelling and less problematic than in the above-mentioned disputations, suggests a disappointing answer to these questions. With nothing in common but hyperreality, cultural subgroups are ships passing in the night without running lights.

A less extreme example of fragmentation is close to home. Political science, in the lifetime of some of us, was once a discipline, a monistic world of commonality. It had a solid (now mythical) epistemological base in logical positivist philosophy of science. It had a set of methods called behavioralism, justified by that base. It had a shared problematic and typical queries presented to it from shared benign assumptions about the American polity (see democratic accountability feedback loop in chapter 1). No matter what one's specialty was, or was evolving toward, there were common landmark books, concepts, and hall-of-fame authors duly anointed to be presidents of the American Political Science Association. Only a very few legitimate journals were read by everyone, and publishing in them was the ticket to national recognition, prestige, and tenure. We submit that political science is no longer a discipline in the sense just described. Its "reality" has thinned as it base was discredited, its methods challenged, its comfortable cognitions themselves made problematic both by events and by powerful intellectual criticism stemming from within.

Political science is now an umbrella term, like a freeway turnoff sign leading to a mall filled with specialty shops, under which an increasingly fragmented series of groups meet. Public administration, in turn, has spun off its own subcategories. The proliferation of sections, similarly multiplied in all learned societies, is evidence of this. Separate journals have sprung up to accommodate diverse specialties, methodologies, and even ideologies. Under conditions of disciplinary fragmentation, it is scarcely possible to have a national hall-of-fame reputation like, say, Schattschneider or V. O. Key. We now have international reputations among networks of approximately eighty similarly engaged scholars who have read, appreciate, and cite our work. We would guess that people from one group, say urban politics, rarely have serious substantive discussions with those from other groups, say international relations formal modelers. Members of different specialties do not read the same material, keep up with the same journal, or get excited by the same new landmark book. Indeed, it is not rational to be a generalist. One can have intense and detailed knowledge of no more than two sub-subfields to which one speaks and in which one is published. Is it not ironic that the only books we have in common are gimmicky introductory texts?

To be sure, the development of disciplinary fractions is not necessarily evidence of insurmountable paradigmatic incompatibility of the type described by Kuhn. A more accurate label might be quasi-incommensurable. Separated, tribalized discourse communities can isolate themselves from one another by inattention and disdain as much as by paradigmatic dissonance at a fundamental epistemological level. The more an individual's identity is connected to a subcultural fragment, the more is this identity replaced with more precise social formations—"urbanist" or "modeler" replaces "political scientist"; devotional replaces Christian; gay man replaces middle-class American. The potential result of neotribalism is that the micropolitics of identity affirmation replaces more generalized national and international will formation. As Jameson (1991, 17) put it: "The stupendous proliferation of social codes today into professional and disciplinary jargons (but also into the badges of affirmation of ethnic, gender, race, religious, and class-factional adhesion) is also a political phenomenon, as the problem of micropolitics sufficiently demonstrates."

Symbolic Politics

The citizens of hyperreality are not so much informed as bombarded with fleeting images designed mainly to manipulate consumers. Emblematic of the monologic communication that now characterizes the public conversation, TV yields up a hyperreality of commodities and symbols that only monied interests can afford to sustain. The barriers to these communications outlets are substantial; campaigns costing hundreds of thousands of dollars represent the minimum ante for a national issue or office. The viscosity of "reality" thins as TV reality, the monologic tendency of hypercommunication, ascends.

Symbolic Politics Ascendant

To declare that elites manipulate symbols does not require postmodern critique; but the interaction between modernist symbol manipulations and postmodern simulated politics is worth investigating. Murray Edelman (1964, 1971, 1977, 1988), whose symbolic politics is grounded in modernity, has been the leading theorist of symbolic politics in political science. Symbolic politics assuages the less powerful while the rewards of material policy, the important stuff, abounds to the benefit of the influential, the organized, and, what makes these possible, the monied classes. By this analysis, the rhetorical preambles to legislative bills (e.g., save the family farm) are developed for unanalytical popular consumption. Obversely, the fine print and subclauses encompass the distributive policies benefiting agribusiness conglomerates. This was an analysis that fit the conditions of high modernity. And, however distorted in favor of organized interests, policy actually did build freeways, electrify the national outback, and construct the suburbs. With all its faults and skews, it was real government. Orthodoxy may have needed reform, but it had legitimacy and truth value. That has changed.

Symbolic Politics Then and Now

So what is new? Politics has always been symbolically mediated. Only rarely have we ever experienced politics directly. Even if a politician were to kiss our baby, eat our ethnic food, or wear our funny hat, that would be symbolic. Certainly, post–Civil War politics, when the "bloody flag of rebellion" was for decades waved, were symbolic. And very little in the name of concrete governance (problem solving) came from these symbols (Sundquist 1973). Reification (taking symbols or names as if they were real objects from nature) has been part of the human condition since the dawn of civilization. But something changed. Modernity, however reified the explanatory systems used to justify it, had more stable metanarratives. And these were at least vulnerable to evidence of internal contradiction. There were truth functions available for use by opponents as well as proponents of the status quo.

To bring out the difference, we contrast the view of Frankfurt School philosopher Herbert Marcuse (especially *One Dimensional Man,* 1964) with an analog from hyperreality. Pretend, counterfactually, that there is a central intelligence steering mechanism for those classes of people (*the establishment* in Marcuse's terms) advantaged by the status quo. In a modern strategy, the advantaged might have conspired in their clubs, universities, and think tanks to come up with some (hegemonic) system of thought, some logically consistent and relatively stable metanarrative of the world by which the relationships of its parts might, however falsely, be grasped, held, and therefore legitimized. And this metanarrative would be flexible enough at its boundaries to co-opt and absorb potential aspects of opposition by reinterpreting them in its own terms. That is essentially Marcuse's theory of one-dimensionality, reducing everything that is other to the unidimensional terms of the monolithic metanarrative. Thus, wearing old jeans as a gesture of resistance to consumerism is co-opted when the market provides new "worn" jeans at premium prices. Marcuse's description still resonates; certain rituals of policy pronouncements, like the State of the Union address, still call for metanarrative co-optation. But modern co-optation has been mightily augmented by postmodern strategies.

In hyperreality, that same counterfactual central intelligence steering committee (the establishment) would have a different strategy—although the goal of gaining acquiescence of others to the favorable status quo would be the same. The establishment would not rely on the old stable metanarrative (of which orthodoxy was a part), because even by the skewed standards set by such a metanarrative, the status quo is amenable to devastating critique. Instead of rescuing the metanarrative, hyperreality makes it easier to continuously divert attention from narratives altogether. Explain not the poverty level, blighted cities, environmental crises, the war, and rates of unemployment or incarceration. Float instead an inexhaustible sequence of unrelated images that pander to more primal fears. Develop instead an endless series of diversionary "plastic disposable reifications" (Fox and Miller 1993) to serve as short-lived, prepackaged conceptual gimmicks that evaporate when opened. Plastic disposable reifications are floating-away helium-filled signs that do not refer to anything concrete. Instead of promulgating ideological pamphlets, traffic in images that can be endlessly reproduced when their freshness or media shelf life has expired. The images are flexibly utilized, intended to last only as long as the typical

TV attention span, yet they present themselves as constitutive of meaning. We suggest that this was the insight of the Reagan-Bush-Atwater public relations presidencies, advanced to the level of genius in the Bush-Cheney-Rove White House.

The Struggle for Meaning Capture

We neither claim nor think in terms of a conspiracy theory where all actors know what they are doing and where they fit into some master plan. Yet we do want to suggest that something like what is described in the previous subsection is happening. Lakoff (2004) starts his book with the example of the term *tax relief* as used by the Bush administration. "Think of the framing for *relief*. For there to be relief there must be an affliction . . . . When the word *tax* is added to *relief*, the result is a metaphor: Taxation is an affliction" (3–4). And, of course, soon after, the news media were using the phrase *tax relief*, and before too long, even the Democrats were using the term. "The conservatives had set a trap: The words draw you into *their* worldview" (4).

Hence, a number of players do have resources. Campaign advisers, bureaucratic elites, journalists, ad creators, political consultants, and intellectuals employed in think tanks or academic institutions have voice. Because the services of individuals practicing these crafts are compensated, it is not unreasonable to assume that those with the power to pay will have asymmetrical capacity in the struggle for meaning capture. Brought into doubt by manipulated symbolic communication is the very possibility of the sequence: rational discourse, leading to popular will formation, leading to governance aimed at ameliorating societal problems.

With individuals no longer possessed of democratic agency, it becomes increasingly difficult to find out who is doing the talking. The era of corporate free speech provides a poignant example.

Corporate Talk

One must first anthropomorphize a corporation before one can accept the notion that a reified abstraction such as corporation or any other human structure (organization, department, religion) can actually speak, as if it were a person having a discussion with other persons. The notion is preposterous at first blush, because only people have larynxes and the necessary vocal musculature to carry out such a task. More to the point, the notion that some individual enters the discourse to speak "on behalf of" a social-structural contraption brings into question the veracity of the speech act.

Entities as Citizens

Treating corporations as if they were citizens has helped to solve public disputes that have cropped up before. In the 1837 Supreme Court case *Charles River Bridge v. Proprietors of Warren Bridge*, organizations (corporations, municipalities) were granted legal status equal to that of an individual citizen for most purposes. Although he lost the case defending a monopoly company against what the courts perceived as the public interest, Daniel Webster successfully argued on behalf of Charles River Bridge that corporations were to be considered "persons" with respect to the privileges and immunities clause in Article IV of the U.S. Constitution, which granted citizens of one state "the privileges and immunities of the citizens in the several states."

The legal status of the corporation was secured. Justice Roger B. Taney, writing for the majority, stated, "We think it is well settled that by the law of comity among nations, a corporation created by one sovereignty is permitted to make contracts in another, and to sue in its courts, and that the same law of comity prevails among the several sovereignties of this Union" (quoted in Janosik 1987, 69). Hence the term *citizen* in Article III of the Constitution has been interpreted to mean that corporations, municipalities, and other organizations are deemed to be citizens; and corporations are endowed by their charters with legal existence as entities.[2] As a result of the case, it became clear that states could legislate against corporations for the sake of the public interest, a victory for the Jacksonian democrats. However, the establishment of the right of corporations to do business in other states and to enjoy the protection of laws was less noticed. The latter point is the more important one for our consideration, because the American legal system from that point on overtly recognized entities such as corporations as citizens, for most intents and purposes.

In 1978 this corporate right of free speech was extended to allow corporations to influence electoral ballot questions, in *First National Bank of Boston v. Bellotti*. The U.S. Supreme Court, in a majority opinion written by Justice Lewis Powell, overruled the Massachusetts Supreme Court. At stake was whether a Massachusetts statute forbidding electoral ballot expenditures by banks and business corporations was a violation of the First Amendment, and the U.S. Supreme Court voted to expand corporate privilege regarding ballot politics.

Whatever the advantages of treating corporations as entities for purposes of economic dispute resolution or electoral politics, the practice does nothing to enhance the public discourse. The speaker, if a corporation, is disembodied and therefore anonymous, and incapable of adopting a standpoint more intangible than utilitarian interest. Whoever utters the corporate claims is necessarily a "mouth organ" and therefore suspect as a willing, attentive participant.

The monologic form of communication is linked to rationally organized, bureaucratized language. In the public sector, its system of hierarchical, superior-subordinate relations displaces the sort of empathic relationships with clients that social workers, for example, might have preferred. The words that the bureaucrat must use are separate from the intentions of the speaker; the individual functionary need not be personally committed to his or her words. There is no point in blaming the functionary for this. There is policy and procedure, but no dialogue with the client. Importantly, there is no struggle to redefine a problem. The job of all organizational functionaries is to work; dialogue, meetings, and further discussions are regarded as sources of friction, chaos, and malperformance. The modern organization snuffs out communal or dialogical communication in favor of the dominant mode of message transfer, which is monologic. Organizational culture thus promotes a social discourse of one-way utterances, unchecked by the possibility of immediate retort.

Suppression of Discussion Regarding Public Concerns

With corporate entities snatching free speech rights, it should be no surprise that Bunnatine H. Greenhouse, a Senior Executive Service contracting official with the U.S. Army, was demoted for criticizing a large, noncompetitive contract with the Halliburton Corporation and its subsidiary Kellogg Brown & Root. She opposed granting of a waiver of the usual competitive bidding process (Eckholm 2005a). She called the contract "the most blatant and improper contract abuse I have witnessed during the course of my professional career" (A9). She was referring to a five-year contract for oil field repairs potentially worth $7 billion—a contract based on a plan drawn up by the same company that was awarded the contract (Eckholm 2005b). Her contesting of corrupt practices went against the hegemony of the top-down monologue.[3]

At the behest of the organizational chain of command, criticism of in-place practices is thus made to be a problem for the criticizer. In another example of organizational monism, Frederick A. Black, a U.S. prosecutor in Guam, was reassigned from Guam, effectuating a shutdown (temporarily, as it turned out) of a criminal investigation of Jack Abramoff, a powerful lobbyist and Republican donor (Shenon 2005). Black's colleagues had to speak to the *New York Times* off the record because U.S. Justice Department rules forbid its employees from talking to news reporters. The suppression of public discussion by agency officials leaves the public with a distorted public sphere, hobbled by the inability of their civil servants to raise their voices. At the FBI, Sibel Edmonds, a translator who had complained that terrorism-related intelligence was not being translated properly—to the point of espionage—was dismissed from her position (Greenhouse 2005). The Justice Department's inspector general found evidence in support of her claims and that the FBI refused to take them seriously, yet the U.S. Supreme Court upheld her termination from the agency. Bottom-up communication is not permissible.[4]

Political Propaganda

Top-down communication, on the other hand, is a different matter. Consider this report of Barstow and Stein (2005):

> "Thank you, Bush. Thank you, USA," a jubilant Iraqi-American told a camera crew in Kansas City for a segment about reaction to the fall of Baghdad. A second report told of "another success" in the "drive to strengthen aviation security"; the reporter called it "one of the most remarkable campaigns in aviation history." A third segment, broadcast in January, described the administration's determination to open markets for American farmers. To a viewer, each report looked like any other 90–second segment on the local news. In fact, the federal government produced all three. (A1)

The prepackaged *news-ready-to-see* format is well known in the corporate world, and now these business practices, like so many others, are being adopted by government. News media have a long history of simply reprinting corporate press releases and video clips. For example, the Sunday Style "feature article" might be a puff piece on that wonderful red sauce sometimes called ketchup and sometimes catsup. Somewhere near the end of it, the reader will be offered a delicious meat loaf recipe that calls for—no surprise—one half cup of <YourBrandHere> ketchup! Clipping services are then hired to read through all the newspapers to which the press release was sent in order to give the marketing department feedback on its efforts to promote the product. In the updated, snazzy TV versions of the practice, fake reporters who look just like real reporters are hired to recite the corporate or (now) governmental message. These government- and corporate-produced "news" reports are played and replayed without attribution on local "news" shows.

We have linked orthodoxy to epiphenomenal symbol manipulation, calling into question the democratic claims of the loop model. Hyperreality also (therefore) brings distress to neoliberal, constitutionalist and communitarian alternatives.

Hyperreality Versus the Alternatives

Neoliberalism as Free Market Sloganeering

Neoliberalism, and the market-style managerialism it advances, at face value and as described by proponents, means the adoption of organization practices that lead to flatter structures, performance measurement, results-orientation, interorganizational networks, and government limited to the value-creating functions it performs best, and with fewer employees.

But this definition undergoes a conical sweep as the precession of simulacra circulates around new meanings. Critics point out that the desirability of the neoliberal program is contestable, and the results of its emphasis on performance measurement have not made government work better, cost less, or made the workplace more democratic for those in it. If a government that costs less works better, the government that costs nothing should work perfectly! The well-publicized failure of FEMA to come to the aid of the people of New Orleans in a timely manner after hurricane Katrina served as a notice that good government does not happen automatically. Moreover, the revelations of corrupt practices by Halliburton and its subsidiary KBR in Iraq serve as reminders of the dangers to the public treasure of contracting out. So-called management reforms serve to disguise, through symbol framing, the corrupt practices. Rent-seeking behavior in the neoliberal mode is carried out

not by bureaucrats but by private corporations. As hyperreal epiphenomena, the so-called management reforms are but a series of self-
referential consulting gimmicks, with shelf lives of about a year or so
each, as the latest management fad moves from "privatization" to "reinventing government" to "new public management" to "contracting out."
A self-aggrandizing fake, the slogan "Run government like a business"
has become another vacuous sign of hyperreality, referring adoringly to
the celebration of "business values" but not much else.

Foundationalism of Constitutionalism

As a constitutionally grounded agency, the Public Administration of the
Blacksburg tendency is the sort of universalizing claim or grand narrative
that postmodernism posits as incredulous. Foundationalist claims are but
strategically crafted metanarratives. At an intellectual level, anything that
attempts to pass itself off as canonical (like the founding of a constitution
or some distant social contract) will be debunked, deconstructed, and dismissed. Such reifications as *sovereignty* are readily dismissed as hyposta-
tized narrative, claims that cannot be redeemed except by self-reference
to one's own particular canon. If constitutionalists assert one version of
the founding, the Iroquois can provide a different narrative of how the
Constitution came to be. (That is to say, what white Americans take to be
the founding was but a plagiarized version of the Iroquois governance
structure.) As reality continues to mutate rapidly, institutions from a different time, articulated for a different set of purposes, will be dead weight.
Institutional endurance may depend not so much on legitimacy as on the
deadlock of a political process unable to develop enough power to jettison
the old institutions—not what the constitutionalists had in mind. The critiques of canon that may be applied to constitutionalism also apply to
orthodoxy, only more so, because orthodoxy has actually done its service
as a dominant metanarrative.

Another metanarrative that has performed service is sovereignty, which
comes across as another reified artifact, an attempt to create the illusion
of certainty.

Community as Sovereign

To the extent that "community" replaces "elected officials" in the
communitarian/civism model, the loop model remains essentially in-

tact, and the bureaucracy can obey a new sovereign, just as Woodrow Wilson imagined an administrative science would do, neutrally serving republicans, monarchs, or whatever master. Community, as reified integer, fits just as nicely as any of those. All these legitimizing gambits sanctify their own sovereignty and impute to it a higher reality, the effect/intent of which is to institutionally outmaneuver competing claimants.

The strategy of advocates of communitarian/civism is not necessarily to reify an artifact as sovereign, although its unexamined references to *the people* might not withstand close scrutiny. Our reading is that community is more often intended as a cultural development toward egalitarian participation and interaction. But community-as-cultural-development presents a different sort of difficulty if the development of community tends toward incommensurability.

Communitarians want all citizens to be involved because the involvement itself is essential to the full development of their potential as humans. Here community exists as a problematic, not as a done deal (or reified artifact). It needs to be nourished, tended to, and developed. Communitarianism assumes universality, that everyone will be able to communicate from their different-yet-similar-enough vantage points. But the existence of similar-enough vantage points has now been called into question. All universals are greeted atheistically. The public conversation is not necessarily, therefore, a war of all against all; it is just not about anything in particular. In his book on postmodernism and democracy, Botwinick (1993) noted Oakeshott's (1991, 489–90) commentary about this sort of conversation: There is no inquiry, no debate, no agreed-upon grounds for asserting truth claims, no propositions to be tested, no persuasion, no refutation, and no requirement that words connote the same thing for everyone. At the lively moments in these conversations, gladiators from factions and various NIMBYs will set out with rigidly fixed points of view and rote scripts to deadlock public hearings and prevent deliberative democracy. Hence the neotribes of hyperreality, unable to communicate effectively one subculture with another, are unable to rescue mass society, or to raise the viscosity of the thin, macrolevel hyperreality, or to provide the universal grounding that would transcend neotribalism.

Better to have participation than not, we continue to agree. But in hyperreality the responsible communitarian citizenry seems ever more absent and lacking, perhaps altogether inaccessible. When community is reduced to a series of otherwise atomized individuals brought together usually by the coincidence of their consumptive activity, the community does not develop political skills. New England town meetings may evoke nostalgic fantasies of true democracy, but these meeting-goers are not participants. Most of the attendees sit quietly amid a roomful of quasi-strangers and listen to whoever possesses the microphone. The town hall meeting turns out to be another serialized community. Communitarians can create a new Department of Citizen Participation whose mission it is promote community involvement, but it matters not what the community is involved in. Alas, communitarians are like gamblers: What matters is not the gain or the loss of money; the thrill is in the wagering.

A Place for Discourse?

Is hyperreality insurmountable? We do not want to be associated with some structurally deterministic position that claims we have crossed over some bridge into a fragmented, relativistic, image-laden, value-deprived, identity-confused fantasy world, with no possibility of return. We would, however, opine that to whatever extent hyperreality, thin national culture, and neotribalism have validity, orthodoxy and the representative democratic accountability feedback loop are more unsatisfying still, if that is possible, than when we left them at the end of chapter 1. Neoliberalism in another time would be dismissed as an elite-run bourgeois profiteering scheme. The alternative of constitutionalism likely would be unconvincing in an era hostile to canon. Likewise, the idealism of communitarianism, although attractive, seems misplaced given citizen indifference and the questionable status of community.

Citizen participation in government would likely be surpassed by the other side of the coin, government participation in the citizenry, if we read Foucault aright. In the next chapter we will begin constructing an alternative theoretical framework that affirms democracy, on the one hand, and can do so in conditions of hyperreality, on the other. In chapter 4 the radical contingency of government as a social construction and as a set of techniques is explicated, with the help of Anthony Giddens and Michel Foucault, among others. The contingency thesis will be extended into chapter 5, where we take practical impasses and symbolic events to be important history-making moments. Hence, in the next two chapters we set about the task of theorizing anew.

Notes

1. Kauffman (2005) found that veterans' charities in the United States spend next to nothing on veterans' causes while contracting out or otherwise diverting 90 percent of their monies to administration and fund-raising. With professional solicitors keeping 70 to 90 percent of the take, the importance of symbolic manipulation (e.g., advertising and marketing) as an economic priority lies just beneath the understandable outrage that this finding elicits.

2. See *The Guide to American Law*, 1983, vol. 2, 325, and vol. 8, 132.

3. Similarly, Captain Ian Fishback told Human Rights Watch that military investigators pressed him to name others who had also gone public with their knowledge of prisoner abuse in Iraq. Fishback has been told that he faces criminal prosecution if he refuses to provide names of others who reported abuse (Schmitt 2005).

4. Perhaps the exception proves the rule. Defense Secretary Donald Rumsfeld, at a press briefing with General Peter Pace, said to reporters "Any instance of inhumane behavior is obviously worrisome and harmful . . . but I don't think you mean [U.S. service members] have an obligation to physically stop it; it's to report it." General Pace, as chairman of the Joint Chiefs of Staff, was able to contradict the secretary by saying, "Sir, they have an obligation to try to stop it" ("Soldiers Told to Intervene" 2005).

4

The Social
Construction of Government

Criticism, at its best, should make it more difficult to do those things that are now too easy. Our excursion into hyperreality in chapter 3 was meant to raise more doubts about the easy rationalistic habits of public administration. With this chapter we now begin our attempt to build a new framework for public administration as an academic field of study. Our first move is to take a radically contingent look at social institutions. We boldly claim that bureaucratic practices come into being via habits of mind, as embodied through work. The first section lays out a social constructivist framework that gathers in Anthony Giddens's decentered idea that institutions are constituted as recursive practices. The second section puts an exclamation point on such decentering by proffering governmental rationality not as an institutionally encumbered entity but, following Michel Foucault, as a technique of power that functions to control, and care for, the population.

Constructivist Social Theory

The reality constructing business has gained considerable prestige since the publication of Berger and Luckmann's *Social Construction of Reality* (1966). To aid students of public administration in classifying this alternative to positivism and behaviorism, we will simply call it constructivism.

Constructivism has this straightforward message for students of public organization: Organizational reality, what public administrators experience as the flux and flow of daily life, is socially constructed. Because organizational reality is not imposed by some impersonal or material force outside of human groups, it is amenable to adjustment by human groups. The word *bureaucracy* only partially connotes what public administrators do, only partially describes the way they do it, and fits scarcely at all with the aspirations of actual public administrators. To say such things credibly, we need to break through the conceptualizations surrounding *bureaucracy* and *institution,* to see what they are made of.

Ontology is about being or existence. The flip side of ontology is *epistemology*, which is about what and how humans might know or acquire knowledge of being or existence. Traditionally—that is, in the history of philosophy—the two are separated, even as tradition affirms that they imply each other. For the social world of everyday life, a constructivist view combines/telescopes ontology and epistemology. This move is made possible by the insight that humans who seek to know social reality are themselves the carriers of it. Observers of social reality cannot be external to it, nor can their observations be incorrigibly isolated from the social phenomena being observed. Conceptions of this reality are in a sense negotiated. This is called the social construction of reality by Berger and Luckmann (1966), and their hugely influential book by that title is what gives constructivism its name.

Accordingly, a constructivist epistemology/ontology is radically nominalist. The names that interactive human groups give things are ultimately arbitrary. They could be any combination of grunts, tongue clicks, and gestures. Names and symbols are not so much denotative of something as they are socially agreed-upon gestures, various shorthand significations for commonly accepted phenomena for which significance has been mutually developed.

Constructivism and Structuration Theory

We cannot simply ignore agencies, institutions, bureaucracies, and constitutional regimes, but we need a way of talking about them that avoids making them into immutable things. According to Weber (1946, 228), "Once it is fully established, bureaucracy is among those social structures which are the hardest to destroy." But organizational structures may be more malleable than Weber supposed. As sociological theorist Anthony Giddens (1984, 26) remarks: "The reification of social relations, or the discursive 'naturalization' of the historically contingent circumstances and products of human action, is one of the main dimensions of ideology in social life."

Giddens wants to avoid ascribing to human constructions the immutability that makes institutions seem like granite mountain ranges. There is a way of accounting for systematics without demeaning the subject-active-voluntarist side required for constructivism. It can be found in the theory of structuration brilliantly developed by Giddens (1984, 2): "One of my principle ambitions in the formulation of structuration theory is to put an end to each of these empire-building endeavors. The basic domain of study of the social sciences, according to the theory of structuration, is neither the experience of the individual actor, nor the existence of any form of societal totality, but social practices ordered across space and time."

Recursive Practices

Crucial to structuration theory is an understanding of the term *recursive*, reoccurring time and again. Recursive is related to habit. Recursive activities "are not brought into being by social actors but continually recreated by them via the very means whereby they express themselves as actors" (Giddens 1984, 2). Humans are born into a world already rich in meanings, which they take up, and in doing so re-create, or reproduce, them, although never exactly identically, for the present and into the future. Humans exhibit reflexivity (i.e., self-consciousness of actions and intentionalities) about their recursive habitual practices. Reflexivity is not applied in a vacuum, but within the flow of action and interaction within determinable limits. These limits are formed by the expectations of others and cocreated by competent selves grasping, accepting, and performing within the limits of those expectations. Such competent performances reinforce and validate those limits, which become structures of varying strength and duration.

Although recursive practices channel and limit human creativity, it is important to also emphasize that they are the occasions for creativity's exercise. Language, itself a pattern of recursive practices, exemplifies the point. Speaking a language means employing particular words and phrases from a rich stock of potential expressions and deploying them according to a more limited stock of grammatical formulae. There are limits to what a particular stock can provide, but it is difficult to imagine, to think outside of that stock (some philosophies would hold it impossible), that which cannot be expressed. Language limits the speakable, but it is also the enabler, the means through which we speak.

Recursiveness only rarely ventures from well-worn paths. Nonetheless, as rivers carve out new beds, so may human behavior in the aggregate change course and incrementally rework recursive patterns.

Such changes, in turn, can and usually do occur as the unintended consequences of marginally adjusted recursive practices aggregated as a social pattern. Governance, and the discursive way of actualizing it, may be regarded as conscious, mutually reflexive attempts at regulating or directing the marginal adjustments of otherwise randomly developing shifts in recursive practices. By this (we think accurate) view, "To say that structure is a 'virtual order' of transformative relations means that social systems, as reproduced social practices, do not have 'structures' but rather exhibit 'structural properties' and that structure exists, as time-space presence, only in its instantiations in such practices and as memory traces orienting the conduct of knowledgeable human agents" (Giddens 1984, 17). In other words, systems, institutions, and the like owe their existence not to some objective realm outside the social practices of individuals in groups, but within them. In short, social reality is socially constructed or constantly socially renewed by human behavior patterns regulated by recursive practice.

We are ready to attach names to recursive patterns of different degrees of duration: Fad and fashion are recursive practices of short and intentionally shifting duration. The joy of variety seems a human trait. Fad and fashion are largely harmless ways to exercise it. At the other extreme, following Giddens (1984, 17), "the most deeply embedded structural properties, implicated in the reproduction of societal totalities, [are called] *structural principles.*" Further, "those practices which have the greatest time-space extension within such totalities can be referred to as *institutions.*"

Institutions Are Habits

Understanding institutions is the most important aspect of structuration theory for our purposes. Following Giddens, institutions are recursive practices sustained by resource appropriation and rules. Rules may be of many kinds, certainly not limited to written rules, laws, or standard operating procedures. Rules may be typed according to their profile across a series of bands between the paired polarities of: intensive-shallow, tacit-discursive, informal-formalized, and weakly sanctioned-strongly sanctioned (Giddens 1984, 22). Notice the potential for variability and ambiguity here. Although they seem stable when viewed as a whole and seen as a cluster of recursive practices, when viewed at a level of detail, one sees microprocesses and particular rules adjusting to interpersonal encounters, to group relations within cliques, and to departmental relations. In other words, one sees the evolutionary transformation of recursive practices amid the details of everyday life. This indeed is precisely the way that specialized jargons develop within groups. Institutions as understood through structuration theory, it follows, are not like institutions of the Weberian ideal type: unalterable slots impervious to the human beings inhabiting them. Such insights are, of course, the stuff of the literature on organizational anthropology.

What we want to stress here is the ever-present potential for institutional malleability. If a given reality is socially constructed, that reality can, and inevitably will, be socially reconstructed. The inevitable evolution of recursive practices usually happens as the result of unintended consequence and the permeability of given clusters of recursive practices to changes initiated elsewhere. But these may also be adjusted by design, as the organizational change movement has shown in countless instances.

Hence any given social construction of reality (i.e., that which gathers up and interactively or reciprocally transforms intentions and projects within groups) may occur within what are now regarded as institutions. This means that the symbols *institution* and *institutionalize* signify contingent, not permanent for-now-and-all-time solidification. The degree of institutional fixity will vary greatly, but it can never be absolute. Institutions are habits, not things. Institutions might look the same from decade to decade from the outside, but their practices must surely vary according to the admixtures of personalities and histories that shape the norms and habits in play within them. From generation to generation the admixture itself will change radically as social sediments shift. Certain gestalt formulations within presumed institutionally fixed structures will actually change the institution itself, even as it goes by the same name and presents for public view the same reified logo. The end result is that "human history is created by intentional activities but is not an intended project" (Giddens 1984, 27).

We have been developing a constructivist standpoint with a structuration amendment because we need to be able to affirm that reified institutions and agencies are transcendable, and also to be able to take into account policy networks, interagency consortia, citizen-agency task forces, and the like. This is because over (often very little) time, these latter nascent socio-political forms also develop recursive practices of sufficient solidity to qualify as instances of institutionalization.

Stable patterns of recursive practices are too often regarded as formations that are a monopoly of bureaus, agencies, and other formal-legal
structures that use the sign *institution* as a synonym for their formal
name (as in "this institution"). Two meanings of institution need to be
kept in mind. Brass-nameplate institutions contain within themselves
many instances of robust institutionalized recursive practices. But relatively stable-over-time institutionalized recursive practices also exist
between brass-nameplate institutions and others of their kind, as well as
under, over, and around them.

We also want to show the permeability of what are often taken to be the
fixed boundaries between public administration—the bureaucracy—and its
clientele (or under the neoliberal spell, its customers). One needs to be able
to draw a distinction between institutions and agencies, taken on the one
hand as boxes on an organization chart written in budget allocations or textbooks, and on the other hand, institutions understood as structurations. Let's
try out our new bag of tricks on bureaucracy. After immanent critique of
bureaucracy, we will be in a position to resituate practices currently thought
of as bureaucratic as, instead, manifestations of discursive events.

Using Constructivism to Deconstruct the "Conflated Aggregation" Bureaucracy

Affirming discourse requires that some old ways of categorizing phenomena be adjusted. *Bureaucracy* is a term that does not capture the
totality of public-sector activity. This term may be regarded as a reified
conflated aggregation, by which we mean a symbol that gathers up diverse and often contradictory events and peremptorily subsumes them
under that symbol. We need to unpack, disaggregate—or in postmodern
terminology, *deconstruct*—the conflated aggregation, the mind-numbing
category, of bureaucracy. For instance, what does it mean, in the debate
over outsourcing of social service, to say that it will decrease bureaucratization? In what way should the conscious discursive attempt to change
some institutionalized recursive practices and promote alternative practices be regarded as bureaucratization?

Properly practiced, deconstruction is no mere tribalistic dismissal of
alien views. It requires a tracing to the roots of a thing, a genealogy or
archaeology, so that they can be laid bare. A genealogy of bureaucracy,
with Weber as chief herald, reveals rational, control-oriented organizations committed to a mechanistic, cause-and-effect deterministic meth-

odology. Subsequent social science amendments to this model posit permeable boundaries. Social constructivism allows the realization that the stuff of bureaucracy is not so concrete and fixed as the closed-system model had supposed. Rather, hypotheses and variables are the constructions of the inquirers or the literature/tradition in which they work.

Formal institutions exist in the context of legitimating value orientations that are both culture-bound and historically contingent, and not at all "objective." Our habits of mind influence the way we see things. Perceptions are easily channeled and ossified when participants, analysts, or managers think that they convey something concrete, whereas the reference is actually to a shared idea—a tacitly agreed-upon set of symbols and expectations. Bureaucracy is not a neutral sign in the marketplace of ideas. Signs guide us in framing what we perceive and already imply a judgment of it. The sign *bureaucracy* enjoys special status in this respect because it not only is an idea in its own right, but, once reified and treated as an objective form, serves as a vehicle for the control and distribution of many other ideas. Yet bureaucracy quite plainly has no objective existence outside of human social interaction.

We want to outflank the concept bureaucracy as if it were but one monolithic way of influencing patterns of recursive practices. Practices are commanded, legislated, forbidden, made criminal or censurable; deviant behavior will result in firing, arrest, or hospitalization. But there is more to it than that. Michel Foucault took the notion of power/resistance, and the context of practice, into areas hinted at by Giddens but unimagined by Weber. Foucault's unit of analysis was not the reified organization; he displayed a Giddens-like sensibility to context and practice in explicating the techniques of power that begins with the analytical parsing of the population into categories, and counting them. While we recognize these as practices of public administration, Foucault was able to present an analysis of techniques of power by focusing not on "the bureaucracy" but on the practices themselves and their functioning in the care and control of the population.

Governmentality

Governmental Rationality

Typical concerns of government are easily recognized by public administrationists: control of epidemics, disease prevention, the food supply, water supply, public sanitation, shelter, education, and so forth. Foucault was interested in *how* government goes about these tasks, and what he finds are technologies of category construction and distinction-making. These are deployed as coherent political technology, a form of political power that began to exercise itself through social production and social service (Foucault 1979). This technology of power made increasing use of categories and distinctions. "[N]ew techniques of power were needed to grapple with the phenomena of population, in short, to undertake the administration, control, and direction of the accumulation of men (the economic system that promotes the accumulation of capital and the system of power that ordains the accumulation of men are, from the seventeenth century on, correlated and inseparable phenomena): hence there arise the problems of demography, public health, hygiene, housing conditions, longevity, and fertility" (Foucault 1984b, 67).

As the population is parsed into categories, things are made to be black or white, and more than that. Whether we like it or not, individuals are counted as members of the population. We are classified: citizen or noncitizen. If classified as citizen, one is called upon to participate, to vote, to grow and develop. On the other hand, we are forced into things: a timetable and a time card for some of us. Soldiers march to the drum. Workers join the rush-hour traffic. One's posture, one's body-position, one's daily bodily comportment are not voluntary. Pupils must sit *just so* if their handwriting is to improve. The body manipulates the machine on the factory floor *just so*. It is forbidden to waste time. Time becomes linear and serialized, organized into successive activities. These are technologies of discipline, the practices of governmentality.

The State.

Governmentality, a term Foucault coined, gives a systematizing meaning to governmental rationality. The systematically employed techniques of public administration/policy are given a rather thorough questioning about what they are up to. By problematizing governmentality, Foucault problematizes the categorization process that presents itself as "scientific." Processes that statistically define the population, for example, are all about governmentality. This kind of governing emerged in sixteenth-century Europe, says Foucault (1979). It was made possible by the creation of specific expert or professional "knowledges." Hence, governmentality came into being concurrently with the societal construction of experts and disciplinary knowledge. How did Foucault come upon this idea?

He went back to the archives and found evidence of an interesting conversation about the state. In a discourse about the art of government, the participants all seemed to be referencing Machiavelli's *The Prince,* which was published in 1513. Machiavelli was concerned with securing a ruler's sovereignty over a state. In subsequent discourse, forty-five years after *The Prince* was published, the people who had read Machiavelli seemed more concerned than ever with the art of government. Some rejected an art of government that focused exclusively on "reasons of state"; others thought Machiavelli had offered a reasonable approximation of what the state demanded; others took strong exception to Machiavelli. But they had something in common. "[W]hat mattered was to keep a safe distance from a certain concept of the art of government, which, once shorn of its theological foundations and religious justifications, came down to the sole interest of the prince as its object and principle of rationality. . . . The essential thing is that they attempted to articulate a kind of rationality which was intrinsic to the art of government, without subordinating it to the problematic of the prince and of his relationship to the principality of which he is lord and master" (Foucault 1979, 7).

Foucault cited as exemplar a 1567 text in which Guillaume de la Perrière asserted that "government is the right disposition of things, arranged so as to lead to a convenient end" (10). Foucault noted that La Perrière did not refer to territory when he spoke of government. "One governs things, but what does that mean? I don't think it is a question of opposing things to men, but rather of showing that government does not bear on the territory but rather on the complex unit constituted by men and things" (Foucault 1979, 11). This definition was momentous, though it would not seem especially profound to the modern reader, whose culture is so thoroughly imbued with instrumental rationality that it is second nature. For Foucault, however, that passage marked a fundamental shift in the way people discussed sovereignty. Before that time period, the object of sovereignty was defined as "the state's preservation, the state's expansion, the state's felicity" (Foucault 1994c, 406). To this new end—the right disposition of things—the easiest and promptest means were to be deployed. The import of La Perrière's text was that it represented a shift away from the exclusive emphasis on the prince and his powers. Hence a new style of political rationality entered the public discourse.

Concomitant with this new concept of the state was the necessity of "concrete, precise, and measured knowledge as to the state's strength. The art of governing characteristic of the reason of state is intimately bound up with the development of what was called, at this moment, political 'arithmetic.' Political arithmetic was the knowledge implied by political competence, and you know very well that the other name of this political arithmetic was statistics, a statistics related not at all to probability but to knowledge of state, the knowledge of different states' respective forces" (Foucault 1994c, 408).

At the moment of this shift in the discourse on the state—when La Pierrière spoke of the right disposition of things—the moment arrived for imagining different possibilities about the role of government. "[I]n the case of government, it's not a matter of imposing laws on men, but rather of disposing things, that is to say employ tactics rather than laws, and if need be use the laws themselves as tactics. To arrange things in such a way that, through a certain number of means, such and such ends may be achieved" (Foucault 1979, 13).

In this literature that Foucault studied, the new art of government was concerned with economy in the same way that households were concerned with economy. The common metaphor was the good father, and what he would do in relation to his wife, children, and servants in making the family prosper—"how to introduce this meticulous attention of the father towards his family into the management of the state" (Foucault 1979, 10).

The point is that government now concerns itself with people, with the population, with people in their relations with each other and in their relations with wealth, resources, and economic survival. Foucault's list of governmental concerns included climate and irrigation, customs, habits and ways of acting and thinking, accidents and misfortunes, famine, epidemics, and death. The dawn of governmentality, then, is a more expansive discourse—compared to Machiavelli—about what it means to provide security for the inhabitants of society. Maintaining territorial integrity remained an important function of government, of course, but to it was added a wide array of other functions that are overtly attentive to the internal conditions of society: production of wealth, provision of the means of subsistence. Hence, the prince's sov-

ereignty or principality gives way to: "A whole series of specific fi-
nalities, then, which are to become the objective of government as
such" (Foucault 1979, 13).

The Rise of Governing

Thus, rather than being largely disconnected from social interactions,
governing becomes the central mechanism for integrating social activities. What constitutes good government? Happiness of individuals becomes a requirement for the state's survival and development.
The *state* and the policies of the state deal not only with people and
their happiness, but with their sociality, with their getting along together, with society itself. Governmentality is about governing a
household, souls, children, a province, a convent, a religious order, a
family.

> From the idea that the state has its own nature and its own finality to the
> idea of man as living individual or man as part of a population in relation
> to an environment, we can see the increasing intervention of the state in
> the life of individuals, the increasing importance of life problems for po-
> litical power, and the development of possible fields for social and hu-
> man sciences insofar as they take into account those problems of individual
> behavior inside the population and the relations between a living popula-
> tion and its environment. (Foucault 1994c, 416)

Foucault is trying to tell us that the emergence of social science, and
we would specify policy science in particular, should be seen in the
context of this new style of political rationality, which should be appre-
hended as a new political technology. Earlier formulations of the state
were generally understood in transcendental terms based on notions of
natural and/or divine law. With governmentality came the view that the
state is governed according to rational principles. This formulation
seemed to prevail until the advent of a series of crises in the seventeenth
century, including peasant rebellions, urban rebellions, and a financial
crisis that affected all monarchies by century's end. The problem of
sovereignty kept asserting itself. So long as the institutions of sovereignty remained the basic political institutions and so long as the exercise of power was conceived as an exercise of sovereignty, Foucault
(1979, 15) wrote, "the art of government could not develop in a specific
and autonomous manner." But when the care and control of the popula-

tion demanded power's attention, the governing of society again became paramount.

The Population

Mercantilism (a term popularized by Adam Smith in reference to European economic thought of 1500–1750) may be understood for our present purpose as an effort to develop the art of government at the level of specific political practices designed to keep the state prosperous. However, mercantilism's objective was not the population, but the sovereign; its objective was not the wealth of the country, but the treasury of the ruler. There is a sense in which mercantilism replayed Machiavelli's focus on the sovereign prince. This older conception for a time displaced, or did not allow in, the as-yet unrealized emphasis on the society—hence immobilizing the development of the art of government temporarily. At the time, contract theory (à la Hobbes, Locke, and Rousseau) placed an emphasis on the relation between the ruler and the ruled, and certainly had a profound impact on public law. But the overarching framework of sovereignty remained strong, and the model upon which the art of government relied—the father and his meticulous attention toward his family—was too weak to make claims about territorial possession or state finance. Hence, the metaphors changed.

The art of government, which once relied on the metaphor of the family as the way of conceptualizing the economy, developed a different basis for contemplating the economy: *the population*. The family remained a valuable unit of analysis, however, because the articulation of demographic data and consumption patterns of the population relied on it. But it was no longer the fundamental model in the art of government. The ultimate end of government had become the population; the effect of this shift was not limited to the family but also affected notions of sovereignty. The aim of government shifted from the power of the ruler to the welfare of the population.

> [P]opulation comes to appear above all else as the ultimate end of government, that is the welfare of the population since this end consists not in the act of governing as such but in the improvement of the condition of the population, the increase of its wealth, longevity, health, etc.; and the means that the government will use to attain these ends are all in some sense immanent to the population, all of them pertain to the population itself on which government will intervene either directly or through large-

scale campaigns, or indirectly through techniques that will make possible, without the full awareness of the people, the stimulation of birthrates, the directing of the flow of population into certain regions or activities, etc. (Foucault 1979, 17–18)

The population thus displaced the sovereign as the end of government. This was the beginning of governmentality, of "absolutely new tactics and techniques" (18).

Tactics and Techniques of Government

The matter of sovereignty remained an acute problem, but the attempt in the West to derive an art of government from a theory of sovereignty was over. Management of the population necessitated the development of discipline. "[I]n reality we have a triangle: sovereignty-discipline-government, which has as its primary target the population and as its essential mechanism apparatuses of security" (Foucault 1979, 19).

And so for Foucault governmentality is constituted by techniques of analysis and reflection, and calculation. While Foucault acknowledges that political theory still concerns itself with the problem of sovereignty, "What we need, however, is a political philosophy that isn't erected around the problem of sovereignty, nor therefore around the problems of law and prohibition. We need to cut off the king's head: in political theory that has still to be done" (Foucault 1984b, 63).

A political theory without the blinders of sovereignty better apprehends how the tactics of governmentality enable a particular power/knowledge formulation whose target is the population. This array of machinery and expertise can be viewed as a type of power, and this type of power is named government. Hence the old European notions of the state have undergone historical change; these changes have transformed the state, indeed have "governmentalized" it. The state itself, in the European tradition, now lacks the importance that is so often attached to it. More important are the tactics and techniques of government, "the only real space for political struggle and contestation" (Foucault 1979, 21). His point boils down to this: Whereas in the olden days, the point of government was to legitimate its sovereign rule, nowadays the art of government entails a different sort of reasoning—to develop competencies and capacities to better solve the problems that arise from the population.

And now, Foucault is urging the development of political theory that thinks outside of sovereignty altogether. This is a very important shift, because political discourse moves from talk about constitutions, the structure of institutions, and legitimate elections to talk about solving problems of the population—which in our view moves political discourse directly to the practices of public administration.

Governmentality, then, is not a theory of the state: it is an analysis of the operation of governmental power, which operates via techniques and practices and rationalities and strategies. It is constituted by rational knowledge of things like public policy, political economy, vital statistics, social statistics, moral and social sciences, and economics. In such a society, the best government translates into *the most economical* government. Particular kinds of power relations are organized through governmental rationality, which has implications for the lives of the governed. Though government (by this we mean in particular public administration and policy science) denies that this is what it does and instead deploys terms such as neutral competence and objective analysis, everything is subject to the power of governmentality.

Foucault's project was to figure out how this happened. And his answer is: By various practices that make human life a domain of power/knowledge. The problems of the population and the techniques of the art of government have become the important practical arena for political struggle and contestation. These modes of inquiry and techniques of government are in no sense neutral. The next subsection, still following Foucault, investigates certain power relations that objectify and discipline the subject.

Subjectification

Classification

Foucault's studies have been an attempt to problematize those modes of inquiry that attempt to give themselves the status of science by objectifying the subject (Foucault 1994d, 326). For example, the medicalization of deviance occurred concurrently with the development of new classifications of disease in the field of psychiatry. How does the social science discourse function? That is the question Foucault posed, and pursuing it enabled him to isolate techniques of governmentality and techniques of power in the social sciences.

There are numerous practices of exclusion that rely on the elaboration of the social sciences that give rise to classification schemes, control possibilities, and containment of segments of the population using humanitarian justifications. Foucault took particular account of what he called "dividing practices" (Foucault 1994d, 326). Taking care of the population meant dividing off the lepers, the poor, and the insane. These divided-off elements of the population were relocated to the hospital or other asylums. The sick were separated from the healthy, the criminals from the good boys. This power was exercised through social science techniques of comparison, differentiation, measurement—dividing off.

The Reductionist Individual

The individual is an essential ingredient for social science, and hence for the techniques of governmentality. In statistics, the individual is normalized through processes of analytical technique. The social scientist deploys the individual as the primary unit of analysis, from which knowledge of the population is inferred. In the database matrix, the individual is the row, the so-called record. The characteristics of the individual are called variables and are standardized in the columns and a value is assigned to each cell in the table. Each variable can be statistically elaborated, so that norms and standard deviations can be calculated. Each individual record (i.e., each individual) can be precisely evaluated in terms of distance from the mean, which is to say, deviation from the norm. By the end of the statistical analysis, the individual has been constructed as a set of categories that are deemed to be descriptive in varying degrees.

But a mere statistical analysis can render the individual invisible amongst the correlations and significance tests. For Foucault, the function of the statistical norm has the opposite effect: *visibility*. The population norm provides a point of comparison for the meticulous documentation of the individual. Individuals become highly visible through such descriptions and assessments. According to Foucault (1977, 190–91), "These small techniques of notation, of registration, of constituting files, of arranging facts in columns and tables that are so familiar to us now, were of decisive importance in the epistemological 'thaw' of the sciences of the individual." Hence, the way a human being comes to be regarded as a subject, a meaning-giving self, deserves consideration. Through the use of social categorizations and dividing practices, the subject is objectified: the productive or laboring subject in economic analysis; the living subject in natural history or biology. These subjectifications (to use another Foucault shorthand term, which means objectification of the subject) are the very procedures of power and knowledge (power/knowledge). The prisoner whose dossier is compiled for him by the warden is in a passive position with respect to his/her own subjectification. The assistant professor who is compiling his/her portfolio is in a more active position, and is in some ways engaged in the act of self-objectification; or in an optimistic interpretation it might be called self-formation. Both are under panoptic and constant surveillance through various forms of examination and periodic review. There is also a kind of eventual collusion in this process by the subject him/herself. And, indeed, the process is amenable to strategic intervention. The moment of power is at the same time a moment of possibility for resistance. Black becomes beautiful; homosexuals become gay. Speculatively, the rapidly expanding capacity for such redefinitions, via Internet blogs and decentralized communication technology, generates the possibility of resistance to dominant metanarratives (as well as opportunities to affirm dominant metanarratives).

In the meantime, autonomous, strategic acts of self-identity are on most workdays overwhelmed by the organized specification of activities and schedules and the assignment of individuals to specific spaces and ranks. Activities are monitored and descriptions are transmitted. Those evidences that are not revealed through the usual methods of surveillance and description may be confessed to the Employee Assistance Program counselor. Self-improvement plans, lifelong learning, and various other modes of individual salvation enable the individual to achieve the success that is his promise—a promise that is accomplishable within a particular and specific discourse that is culturally and historically situated, there being no objective criteria for fulfilling one's promise. Indeed, the multiplicity of criteria, of potentials, of identities and images of success has taken its toll on the once-robust centered individual.

The subjectified individual has now been parsed into so many marketing strategies (as variables in the prediction of purchasing behaviors), and into database records for information about distribution of retirement benefits, blood type, risk to homeland security, credit worthiness, value-and-lifestyle profiles, and so on. *Homo subjectifiedo* has become a record in a database, retrievable by social security number, driver's license number, arrest record, or purchasing patterns. So precarious is this creature's uniqueness that he is now exposed to "identity theft." Yesterday they stole his blue Schwinn bicycle; today it is his identity. That portion of one's identity not stolen by imposters and not captured in the database has been taken into calmness by Prozac and stimulated to erection by Viagra.

Decentered Subjectivity

Hence, the subject is not a God-given concept but a socially constructed one. How did the construction of subjectivity in terms of individuality come about? The subject is objectified through operations on their bodies, their souls, their thoughts, and through their own conduct (Rabinow 1984, in reference to Foucault's 1980 Howison lectures). As a technique of subjectification, individual identity expresses a mode of self-understanding of a particular sort. Individualization implicates commonality and social concerns, if only to accentuate differences and social conflict. The subject possessed of individuality stands apart from—is objectively distinguishable from—the social milieu that provides a meaningful context for the individual's license to be unique. This is but one way in which the subject is objectified. By drawing attention to subjectification and culturally specific discursive production of the subject, Foucault has challenged the immutability of constructions such as the autonomous, liberal-humanist agent.

The countereffect of Foucault's work on subjectification has been a decentering of subjectivity, away from the incorrigible, autonomous, determinate individual and toward a malleable, culturally constructed individual. According to Howe (2001, 170–71): "Governmentality is a form of power that fits people into a productive system by managing their relations both with one another and with themselves. When circuits of power change, individuals routinely adapt, reeducate, retrain, renegotiate, or reinvent themselves in a quest for both their own and society's security. . . . Governmentality is above all a form of social coordination in which individuals monitor their own behavior and voluntarily facilitate circuits of power."

Few public administration scholars have adopted this view of the dispersed, decentered subject. The passage from Howe suggests that the decentered subject might be hopelessly malleable and formed by techniques of power. Hence, there has been a recent move in the social sciences to reassert the individual, in the form of agency and the body, because it is not evident how the discursive practices of the decentered self will bring about social change (Lenoir 1994). Without the active, robust agent, it is difficult for the Western mind—accustomed to conceptual formulations in which the autonomous individual plays the prominent role—to imagine social change taking place.[1]

Abandoning the image of the efficacious individual need not be a cause for despair. Howe proposes a different way of looking at the system of governmentality and administrative discretion: "It might more profitably be understood as an expanded terrain for democratic contestations" (Howe 2001, 171). It is in this spirit that we take up the problem of symbolization in the next chapter.

So far we have portrayed the reified institution as a set of recursive social practices, bureaucracy as set of habitual comportments, and government as a specific set of techniques put to use in caring for and controlling the population. All of these moves have denied foundational essences to familiar categories. In the next chapter we will relocate whatever essence can be retained in the ideographic events and impasses of cultural communication.

Note

1. From a completely different perspective, a skeptical attitude toward the self-determining agent was well expressed by Francis Crick, who wrote in *The Astonishing Hypothesis: The Scientific Search for the Soul* that "You, your joys and your sorrows, your memories and your ambitions, your sense of personal identity and free will, are in fact no more than the behavior of a vast assembly of nerve cells and their associated molecules" (99). A familiar reaction against skepticism toward the autonomous individual agent is one of anxious defensiveness.

5

Ideographic Discourse

Symbols as Ordering Devices

In the last chapter we introduced Giddens's structuration theory, building on social constructivist thought to put forth a view of institutions as constituted by social practices. Then, drawing from Foucault's genealogy of governmental rationality, we deepened the appreciation of how Western societies articulate and extend norms through techniques of governmentality; in Foucault's view through techniques of normalization, individualization, and subjectification. With a new ontological understanding of public administration's function, we now take an affirming look at the reality-producing function of ideographs—our imaginary, image-generating unit of symbolic coherence.[1]

In ideographic discourse, events are the things that happen when two ships passing in the night collide instead. The vessels that collide are abstract, containing symbolizations and their own sense of appropriate everyday practices. We name these transportive vessels *ideographs,* and we consider the movements, collisions, and contestations of such symbolizations to be a field of politics. An appreciation of symbolization and the potential for marginal adjustment to one's symbolic sympathies is necessary to get at the core of what goes on in ideographic discourse.

The starting point in the appreciation of symbolization is reason. Efficacious though reason may be in figuring out what to do and how to do it, its efficacy must be regarded as limited. Many of us in public administration, public policy, and the social sciences subscribe to an inflated view of rationality; inflated because reason cannot fulfill the desire to know the whole of everything. It cannot describe the universal nor have universal application. The longing for rationality's promise of clarity is the very meaning of Camus's absurdity (Eubanks and Petrakis 1999).

Mead (1967) instead conceptualized symbolic relations as part of a system of actions and saw the social processes entailed in collective action as the starting point for social research efforts.

This works well for those interested in purposive action—which may well include most public administration scholars—though it is not clear that teleological ambitions are necessarily implied by symbolization. Symbols may be tools for pragmatic action, but they are not necessarily so. And this is but one of the many important questions that arise with respect to symbolization.

Schutz (1955) provided the service of raising some others: What is the difference between a sign and a symbol? How does the process of symbolization transpire? What is the relation between the signifier and the signified, or between the symbol and meaning? Schutz saw that individuals experience society, groups, and communities symbolically; later theorists (e.g., Lindahl 1998) see the role of symbolic activity as *domesticating* reality.

Czarniawska (1997) traces the interest in symbolization back to a symbolism movement of the nineteenth and twentieth centuries. "Symbolism stood against fixed meanings, and put symbol in its center as a communicative medium—to communicate between the subjective experience and the social inheritance of a culture, in a play of ambiguity and shifting interpretations which has no definite 'key' or 'code' to it" (154–55). Edelman (1964, 1971, 1977, 1988), has been the leading theorist of symbolic politics in the United States. He made the case that symbols and language matter because "they define public problems, construct political realties, generate political support, and create favorable responses toward governmental actions" (Burnier 2005, 500–501).

Symbols and Metaphors

The problem that Lindahl (1998) sets out to address is this one: "If democracy's reality always falls short of its idea, how and why is the postulate of popular sovereignty a necessary condition for a democratic society?" (12). In other words, why is the relation between democracy-the-ideology and democracy-the-reality such that the idea of popular sovereignty cannot be simply banished as a mere illusion? The answer requires looking again at political power: "Political power is undoubtedly *also* an institutional phenomenon, but institutions are not its primordial locus; the locus of political power is *symbolization*" (Lindahl 1998, 14).

Symbolization has long been regarded as the key to forming a coherent view of self and others. Eric Voegelin postulates an intimate intertwinement between reality and symbols: "The self-illumination of society through symbols is an integral part of social reality, and one may even say its essential part, for through such symbolization the members of a society experience it as more than an accident or a convenience; they experience it as of their human essence. And, inversely, the symbols express the experience that man is fully man by virtue of his participation in a whole which transcends his particular existence" (Voegelin 1952, 27, cited in Eubanks and Petrakis 1999).

Hence, symbolic systems such as language contribute mightily to the shaping of what is taken to be reality. Narrative texts are capable of redescribing the world of practice, the world of the real, and the world of the imaginary—all these worlds are communicated through processes of symbolization. Worlds of narrative description collide with one another. This is what makes symbolization so politically and culturally hazardous. Narrative allows the ordering of the chaos; symbols impose a unity where none existed, and such unities are malleable and changeable, in the same way that reality and culture are.[2]

This chapter culminates our attempt for the field of public administration no less than a *paradigm shift* from bureaucracy to ideography, as potentially eye opening (we hope) to public administration as the very similar shift from Newtonian physics to quantum mechanics has been for physics. We begin with the physics story to show how a change in metaphor can change ontology and epistemology; can change the conceptualization of what is being done; which then changes recursive practices.

Physics and Metaphors

Institutional structures were not always as they appear in their contemporary manifestations, but were created and then modified by practice—by processes of social interchange and ideographic realignment. Physics, too, made its appearance in historically contingent conditions that defined the domain and structure of physical science. Physics was not created whole by some primordial heroic physicist. Physics is a set of evolving recursive practices. Practice and consciousness travel apace.

Different language games orient communicators to different constellations of phenomena and codetermine them. When attention is repaid with interesting results, we seek to communicate our findings. This communication impulse is as true in child's play as it is for science. "Look what I found," we say. Physicists, finding something interesting, appropriated the category *particle* to communicate their findings in atomic research. According to Morçöl (2002), "The ancient Greek philosopher Democritus called such ultimate units of matter *atomos*—literally, 'not able to be cut'—in the 5th century B.C." (121). However, physicists in the twentieth century studying subatomic particles found otherwise. Particles and waves, it turned out, were not mutually exclusive. Particles lost their status as irreducible building blocks, while the phenomena of experiments were signified with metaphors that merged with what was observed. As Morçöl put it, "As quantum physicists have showed many times, experiments designed to detect particles always detect particles; experiments designed to detect waves always detect waves; no experiment shows the electron as behaving as a wave and a particle at the same time" (125). "Furthermore," adds Morçöl (126), "we have to interfere with the atomic processes in order to observe them; therefore it is meaningless to ask what the atoms are doing when we are not looking at them."

Measurement devices such as the electromagnetic microscope, the attention of interested observers, and the categories they selected to communicate their findings became part of the phenomena they studied. In other words, the phenomena were signified with metaphors that merged with what was observed. A classic enigma is illustrative.

The double-slit experiment is well-known among physicists: Imagine a panel with two slits in it, standing in front of a screen. If one of the slits is closed, light enters through the other slit, and a corresponding distribution of light can be observed on the screen. If both slits are opened, the light particles hitting the screen manifest something more peculiar in the aggregate than two distribution patterns summed. A different pattern appears, one that seems impossible if light were truly particulate. The distribution of light on the screen confirmed an alternative hypothesis based on a different metaphor: that light has the properties of a wave rather than a particle. Yet, in other circumstances, light was thought to be particulate. The wave-particle enigma seemed extraordinary when its implications were first perceived, and the enigma remains marvelous and peculiar. The enigma also applies, remarkably, when electrons are used instead of a source of light (Hawking 1988).

An important point was well expressed by Wallace (1989) in his discussion of quantum physics. He explained how a particle has a distinct size and location, and either bounces off other objects or penetrates through them. Waves have three dimensions and spread out. They may pass through one another and can interact to produce interference patterns. Because waves and particles are so fundamentally distinct, it stands to reason that no object can be both . . . but electrons seem to display the qualities of both. How can we account for this? "The enigmatic quality of this discovery may be attributed to an apparently innate tendency of the human mind known as *reification*. . . . On the basis of everyday experience, physicists assumed that the electron is a particle. This form of scientific realism, like everyday realism, ignores the critical role of the subjective instrument of observation" (Wallace 1989, 57–58).

Thus, the everyday atomic particle of classical physics was a creature of human categories, regarded as an independent force with material "thingness." Certain properties were presumed to be intrinsic characteristics of the electron. But different research conditions and different measuring instruments suggested the presence of a wave. Electrons-as-particles are whole, they bounce off other particles, and they are irreducible. Electrons-as-waves merge with other waves and are infinitely divisible. Either category fails, at some point, to convey all that is happening.

Additional research has added more uncertainty. Researchers working on micro-entities found that the type of measurement device used and the setting of the experiment seem to influence the results. Specifically, the velocity of a particle that is being measured can be measured only by disturbing it ("bombarding" it) with a minimum amount of light; hence the more accurate the measurement of speed, the less accurate is the measurement of position (Hawking 1988). This is quantum theory's *uncertainty principle.* Social scientists may recognize a resemblance to the Hawthorne effect, in which the researcher's instrument, or the researcher herself, will produce an effect in the subject that is independent of the experimental treatment (Overman 1991). Inevitably, what we see depends on our sensory perceptions and our instruments of measurement, and use of these tools changes what we see.

Although both the physical and the social sciences are unavoidably reifying, there is a difference worth taking into account. Physical scientists observe microdynamics and name (conceive, reify, conceptualize) the electron and the proton in order to be able to communicate their understanding. When social dynamics are observed, they are named (reified) the husband and the wife or the boss and the subordinate or the teacher and the student. The mere naming of a role brings with it expectations of behavioral compliance with recursive practices. Signifying not only communicates our understanding but normatively conditions relationships; there is an element of prescription. Judgmental aspects of an observation are only rarely bracketed. For example, when Lowi (1993) pronounces that "the assumption of selfish interests is probably the only thing on which all political scientists agree" (262), he is doing more than dismissing those who would disagree (your authors among them) with the atomistic conception of the individual. He is prescribing an outlook, and by doing so offers it as the dominant assumption about human nature.

In the final analysis, however, physicists presuppose ontology, too. Quantum theory showed that the deterministic laws and corresponding picture of the physical world provided by Newtonian physics was inaccurate. Atomic particles did not behave as their laws or prescriptions indicated. Students of quantum mechanics overtly acknowledge the participation of consciousness (attention, intention, instruments of perception, conceptual categories) in the representation of physical reality (Jahn and Dunne 1986). Particles seem like waves; waves seem to communicate among one another; the researcher influences the dynamics under study. How can these anomalous influences be taken into account? Abandoning the atomic particle as the fundamental unit of analysis was the first step.

The purpose of our excursion into physics, often thought of as the hardest or most objective of sciences, has been to show how names and metaphors influence the phenomena. Names for phenomena intrude to become part of the phenomena themselves. Names channel the deployment of our perceptual apparatus. They allow some things to be perceived as phenomena, and have the power to blinder us off to alternative perceptions, although not forever. Changing names, changing metaphors, is therefore no small niggling matter (see G. Morgan 1986). Again, we want to say that an ontological change from reifications such as bureaucracy and toward ideographic events is akin to the change from Newtonian physics to quantum mechanics; in both incidents, we must be prepared to give up the age-old dream of an inherently ordered universe.

Ideography

We are all products of our times. This means that our nature as humans is not fixed and constant, but malleable, changeable, and evolutionary.

Culture, which is constituted by ideographs, varies over time. The definition of an ideograph gathers in concepts such as ideology, myth, symbols, images, and mental pictures that more or less cohere into a meaningful symbol system. The ideograph guides behaviors and beliefs into channels easily recognized by a community as acceptable and laudable, or not. Hence, in public discourse, ideography invokes coherent patterns and recognizable formulations. There is a sense in which ideographic patterns regulate power and weave the texture of reality.

As assimilated into an individual's persona, these meanings, impressions, and symbols constitute his unique personage and shape his subjective reality.

Subjective Reality as Pictured Objects

An *ideograph* may be defined as a symbol used in a linguistic system to represent not just the object pictured, but some thing or idea that the object pictured is supposed to suggest or connote. The term ideograph was employed by McGee (1980) to sidestep some of the baggage that attended terms such as myth or ideology, but also to explicitly link connotative concepts to symbolic systems. "An ideograph is an ordinary-language term found in political discourse. It is a high-order abstraction representing collective commitment to a particular but equivocal and ill-defined normative goal. It warrants the use of power, excuses behavior and belief which might otherwise be perceived as eccentric or antisocial, and guides behavior and belief into channels easily recognized by a community as acceptable and laudable" (McGee 1980, 467).

Hence, in public discourse, ideographic usage invokes patterns of political consciousness. There is a sense in which ideographic patterns normalize reality. The term ideograph involves discursive possibilities for change and contestation. An ideographic structure entails pictures, images, symbols, linguistic impressions, and meaning systems.[3]

In a political mode, the ideograph operates as a field of contestation —similar to what Stone (1988) called "goals" (that is, policy objects such as equity, efficiency, security, and liberty). She described these ideas and portrayals as the stuff of strategically crafted arguments. Her famous example in chapter 2 of the difficulties that arise when attempting to fairly and equitably distribute slices of her chocolate cake illustrates the lack of constancy of any ideograph. An ideograph like *equity* may seem like an obvious injunction for fairness at first glance, but questions immediately arise in any practical context. For example, there is always the question of membership (who is eligible to be treated equitably?). There is the question of criteria: Should equitable distribution be based on need, merit, or some other ranking scheme? And, is the appropriate unit of analysis the individual? Or does membership in a victimized group signal eligibility? The nature of the slices of chocolate cake, and whether a slice should be distributed in recognition of other distributions (glass of milk, cup of coffee, prior ham sandwich) presents further legitimate challenges to the once simple matter of equitable distribution. There are a range of distribution processes that are arguably equitable (e.g., pure competition, pure chance, popular vote), but the choices within the range imply vastly different ways of getting there. Hence, the determinative properties of cultural ideographs are fantastically indeterminate.

Ideograph as Unit of Analysis

Rather than projecting images onto individuals, we could gather them instead into ideographs. In this way, inflated images of autonomous and free-thinking individuals controlling their destinies and enacting social change can thereby loosen their strong grip on the imagination. Individualistic heroism and blame-worthiness have been employed in epic stories, legal arguments, and the distribution of privileges and authority, but these story lines can be written differently. Characteristics projected onto individuals, be they heroes or be they villains, can also be understood as expressions of the culture, with its tragedies, its fissures, its dramatic conflicts, and irresolvable predicaments. Mythical gods might have taken on this function in antiquity.

Readers already prepared to abandon the accounts of history predicated on heroes and masterminds (sometimes ridiculed as "Great Man" accounts of history) will appreciate this approach readily. In Foucault's understanding, "discourse is not the majestically unfolding manifestation of a thinking, knowing, speaking subject, but, on the contrary, a totality, in which the dispersion of the subject and his discontinuity with himself may be determined. It is a space of exteriority in which a network of distinct sites is deployed" (Foucault 1972, 55). Recourse to the individual agent—either a transcendental subject or a psychological subject—as the fundamental unit of analysis is an analytical strategy of the modern era. An alternative strategy is to problematize the seemingly neutral objects, the seemingly neutral rules, and the taken-for-granted modes of relations. Ideography may be understood as such a strategy for problematizing the taken-for-granted.

Derrida and the Reality of the Image

The presumption of a reality-in-itself is one such taken-for-granted neutrality that is problematized in postmodern thought. Derrida (1991, 177) has in mind those instances where "the image *supervenes* upon reality, the representation upon the present in presentation, the imitation upon the thing, the imitator upon the imitated." He wants to turn the status difference between reality and the signifier on its head. Think of the reality of the image—the reality of a myth, an ideology, a television message, a political icon, or any cultural symbol or graphic presentation. Discussing reality as constituted by these sorts of concepts is considerably more encompassing than the reality of fact representation (an important but narrow domain of reality construction). Derrida (1976, 87) wrote of the *graphie* to tease out the more subtle implications for rationality and its fact-representational episteme: "The access to pluridimensionality and to a delinearized temporality is not a simple regression toward the 'mythogram;' on the contrary, it makes all the rationality subjected to the linear model appear as another form and another age of mythography."

In other words, the fact-representational episteme (unidimensional and linear) is posed against the mythogram. But Derrida goes even further; fact-representational, linear reality *is* another mythogram. Problematizing epistemology this way is sure to encounter some problems. As Derrida (1976, 87) was quick to add: "Such a cultural graphology, however legitimate its project might be, can come into being and proceed with some certitude only when the more general and fundamental problems have been elucidated; as to the articulation of an individual and a collective *graphie,* of the graphic 'discourse'— so to speak—and the graphic 'code,' considered not from the point of view of the intention of signification or of denotation, but of style and connotation. . . ."

Phenomenological intentionality and the strong agency of individualism are both dealt a blow in Derrida's writing. A satisfactory articulation of the individual in an ideographic culture remains an unfinished problem, but Derrida predicts that its completion will come in describing the ontology of style and connotation. The complexity of ideography has magnified since 1967 when Derrida's book was published in its original French. Reality and the human grasp of it *decohere* when destabilized symbol-referent relations mutate into hyperreality. It has become evident that television and the Internet have expanded the domain of connotation, and rendered its grasp more difficult as the velocity of electronic circulation has destabilized graphic styles that might once have been regarded as constants.

The reality properties of the ideograph are symbolic. Symbolic representation of reality takes us again to the fundaments of difference: connotation and denotation. The play of difference between connotation and denotation is more apparent in *writing* than in *speech,* according to Derrida (1973). Imagine suspending judgment about something that just happened; deferring, in other words, the moment of correspondence between appearance and reality. This deferring means that both appearance and reality are asked to wait before their correspondence is consummated—a temporal deference. Appearance, which has already been perceived, is asked to wait for reality, which has not yet entered the scene.

When *appearance* is unwilling to defer, unwilling to play the difference between appearance and reality, appearance is taken for reality. Another way of putting it is that reality never arrives at the scene when there is no deferring. This absence of play has been described in other contexts as *mindless empiricism.* If, however, appearance is willing to wait and to defer, the ideographs (Derrida would say *the text*) are allowed to play with perception, to bring reality to bear on the situation. An example is the sunrise, which looks to the eye's appearance like the sun's rising. If this appearance defers, scientific ideographs (credited to Copernicus and Galileo) are allowed to enter the scene. The reality, then, is not the sun's rising but the earth's turning on its axis as it circumnavigates the sun. With deference, the contestability of appearances is allowed to play out.

Where is the location of reality, then? Does it exist "out there" in the empirical world? No. It exists in the ideographs (including Copernican theory) that are inscribed on one's subjective personage. The reality is in the theory, as it were, and not in the perception.

Derrida's *difference* has other implications as well. Reality may re-

side in the ideograph, but the ideograph's meaningfulness becomes coherent through differences that it systematizes. In other words, the meaning is in the difference. Symbols refer to a system of signifiers that differ.
For example, the word *expressway* refers to the other markers in a linguistic system: street, lane, circle, highway, avenue, road. Similarly, the
word *blue* is meaningful because of the things in the system it is not:
red, yellow, green, or orange (Eco 1985).

Is reality therefore an inner phenomenon rather than an external one?
The internal-external difference may not be the difference that matters
here. Ideographs are inner phenomena in that they can be conjured or
imagined, and they can be deeply personal. They are external in that
they are produced, nurtured, refused, accommodated, or reinforced by
general cultural forces. Hence, ideography contains no internal-external
gaps for escaping from reality. Ideographically speaking, the only escape from reality is the sensory empirical, where appearance refuses to
defer, where there is no play. But beware the sense-data empirical world
where coherence-making ideographs are expelled; it is just one dang
thing after another out there! Ideography is the landscape on which patterns develop and reality structures itself into something knowable.

Relief from Dissonance

Symbolization is humankind's safe harbor from the everyday treach-
ery of chance and accident. While Charles Darwin integrated the accidental into the very genetic makeup of all animals, we humans prefer
to deny that this applies to us. Yet there are parts of the world where
lions still surprise humans and eat them, where disease wipes out communities, where tsunamis kill everyone on the island, and where hurricane flooding leaves residents of cities homeless. Dismay over arbitrary
and terrible events can be overcome sometimes with techniques, knowledge, and skills. Science in particular can be assigned credit for developing the methodologies and norms that allow, enable, and encourage
a human confrontation with the arbitrary and accidental. We can never
be sure if we are looking at randomness or patterns we have not yet
learned to recognize. Despite pattern-detecting advances in the natural and social sciences, accident and chance do not thereby disappear.
Accident and chance are capable at any moment of threatening the
fragile psychic coherence that society has manufactured. The struggle
against chance and disorder is not just a scientific quest; it is also a

psychic quest. The closer to random everything appears, the closer to madness everyone feels.

Hence, chance, randomness, and accident tend to be eschewed as error rather than embraced as a welcome part of the equation. The disrespect and suppression of the random may be a mistake.

Grand narratives of recoherence are generated in culture to rescue it from the random. Religion and ideology function to mask the radical presence of—not God or reality-in-itself—uncertainty and ambiguity. Happily colluding in whatever making of sense can be achieved, we humans thus enjoin the struggle for meaning capture.

The Struggle for Meaning Capture in the Public Sphere

The ideograph is not merely a symbol; it is a vehicle for associating or distancing one symbol with another. Most importantly, it is the very backdrop against which politics takes place—the public sphere is made of contestable symbolizations. The contest plays out in the contemporary political and cultural battleground of media-infused ideography, where images are brought together in seemingly violent confrontation. It is not merely a war of words, but a clash of symbols, identities, and images. Senior commanders leading the war in Iraq were quite aware of this when they admitted to planting news in Iraqi newspapers. They hired a public relations firm that translated American propaganda into Arabic as part of the struggle for meaning capture (Schmitt 2005). Some of the rhetoric is purposefully deceptive; some of it is sincere. For those of us on the receiving end, it requires increasingly sophisticated skill to discern meaning and coherence among all the hysteria, confusion, and manipulation.

The Internet encyclopedia Wikipedia exemplifies the democratic breadth of the struggle for meaning capture. Entries are collaboratively written by volunteers. Users are allowed to correct and extend the entries. The result is that wide arrays of voices (though not just anyone) are part of the conversation. With that open approach, well-reasoned, yet sometimes competing, versions of truth are manifestly obvious.

Peter D. Feaver, a Duke University political scientist who became a U.S. National Security Council staff member, had (according to Shane 2005) conducted research showing that heavy casualties in war would be tolerated by the American people if they believed the war would eventually result in victory. The link to this research and President Bush's "plan for victory" speech of November 30, 2005, is an interesting one.[4] The fact that Bush used the word *victory* repeatedly in his speech, which Feaver almost certainly had a hand in writing, is indicative of how the battle for meaning capture is conducted. As an ideograph, *victory* resonates with symbols such as success, triumph, accomplishment, and winning. We can justifiably speculate that the speech was not about fighting the insurgency in Iraq; it was a tactical political maneuver in the battleground known as American public opinion.

Ideographic politics, like hyperreality and symbolic politics, has always been with us; it has only recently been problematized because marketing and public relations have become more sophisticated and communications technology more ubiquitous.

Events, Impasses, and the Authority of the Archives

Metaphors, Frames, and Ideographs

What we have been calling ideographs, Lakoff and Johnson (1980) would call metaphors, and Lakoff (2004; 2002, 4) would call frames, mental models, or an "unconscious system of concepts." All of these attempt to name the phenomena of political and cultural cognition and communication. Lakoff (2004, 17) gets at the idea this way: "Concepts are not things that can be changed just by someone telling us a fact. We may be presented with facts, but for us to make sense of them, they have to fit what is already in the synapses of the brain. Otherwise facts go in and then they go right back out."

This would explain why there are people who continue to believe that Saddam Hussein was linked to Al-Qaeda and the 9/11 attacks. They have a frame, a stereotype, a narrative, an ideographic cognition, or a mental model that cannot accommodate certain dissonant facts. And it is not just "they" who transport ideographs from one event to the next; cognition itself works this way (Lakoff and Johnson 1980). Hence, the paradigm commitments that Kuhn noticed can be linked to processes of cognition. The implication here is that the way to conduct an argument is not at the factual level, or even the experiential level, but at the ideographic level.

Ideographies collide with one another, but it is a collision that takes place with relevance to social practices. The confrontation of ideographs, one with the other, constitutes the way we think and the way we act. In public administration the gap between "theory" and "practice" is much discussed, but ordinarily not as contesting ideographies.

Theory/Practice

Theory is an ideograph-like symbolization that claims for itself a high level of coherence and generality. Theory connects interdependent events, or lays out some ideal, or proposes an explanation. Theories contain propositions that are at least somewhat coherent, and perhaps may be parsimonious and systematically articulated. Theory is often dismissed because its aspiration for coherence renders it abstract and therefore irrelevant by those who work in the so-called real world of practice. We need to take a look at what is going on here, in light of what Giddens has taught us about recursive practices.

The word *practice* implies the repeated performance of work. By relying on habit (and hence on prevailing categories of understanding), the practitioner may think that theory has nothing to do with his actions. However, she enacts an ideograph through practice in much the same way that a theoretician accepts a paradigm. The practice/paradigm becomes second nature as it becomes habit. Its premises and presuppositions are no longer problematic. The comfort level has risen. Change in practice/paradigm is not impossible, but it would entail certain psychic and practical inconveniences—like learning a new word processing program.

According to Gherardi (1999, 313), "Competence development can be conceived as the symbolic transformation which emerges from the modification of practices, of meaning systems, and of thought . . . ." Change processes are symbolic fields, entailing both the aspiration for amelioration and the fear of destabilization. Competence, by this view, is a symbolic domain, "an imaginary territory comprising the ideas, projects and emotions that subjects attribute to their organization with a metaphorical map which represents organizational life" (316). The point can be generalized to any process of changing practices, without necessary reference to competence. The possibility of change presents itself, in both theory and practice, when there is an impasse that invokes both aspirations (for amelioration) and fear (of destabilization).

The Impasse

At the workplace, most of everyday life is habitual, and most of us like it that way. We do not want to have to renegotiate each next moment from scratch. We like to know what to expect from one another. Doing everything differently every day would be disorienting. There are regularities in practitioners' work lives because of the patterns generated through daily practice. When we go to work, we carry with us certain expectations of others and bring knowledge of the routines we learned yesterday or last year. This predictability of everyday practices is what enables long-term cooperative projects and makes reality seem like an orderly thing.

However, at some moment a practitioner becomes aware that old habits no longer work. It could be that the environment has changed. It could be that the problems that old practices were designed to solve have disappeared or changed. It could be that better ways are available, and one has only now become aware of them. It could be that we ourselves have changed, and can no longer tolerate the old ways. In any case, the old ways no longer seem appealing. We have reached an *impasse.*

This is a moment where ideographs collide. We have reached an impasse and the old ways no longer work for us. We must think anew. We must do things differently . . . but how? At this moment we can see how the old ways were based on conceptualizations of the real world that no longer seem adequate. These conceptualizations are made of images, symbols, sentiments, ideographs, and so on. The old ways once seemed like second nature, but they cannot have been the only way to do things. Now that they no longer work as we want them to, they are seen as impractical. What is needed at this moment is a new theory.

Hence, practice may be understood as theory-in-place. It is a conception of appropriate action that is informed by ideography inscribed through training, supervision, and prior sense making. And theory is, at least potentially, *practice-to-be,* waiting to be enacted once it is connected to appropriate circumstances. Theory is an understanding of the world that awaits an impasse, an event, a moment of enactment. Practice, often expressed through bodily movements, has become second nature and no longer seems to require any abstraction whatsoever. Practice can change, but it requires effort and political contestation between and among ideographs at the moment of impasse.

The impasses are conflicts between ideographs. The conflict can be between one practice and another practice (as between the practices of the accountants and the practices of the budget analysts; or the practices of the auditors and those of the program evaluators; or the practices in-place and those recommended by an outside adviser; or an old identity as opposed to a new attractive one). Impasses occur not when status quo practices suffice, but when they are contested in some way. These impasses are like anomalies in Kuhn's (1970) sociology of science. As poorly explained anomalies accumulate, the pressure to retheorize mounts.

To say that practical impasses function like anomalies in science is to cast both theory and practice into the realm of ideographic contestation. One might wonder where all this ideographic weaponry is stored. To borrow a Foucauldian term, the ideographs are stored in the archives of cultural and personal histories.

The Archive

The everyday meaning of archive conjures up images of a sort of library, where documents, official memoranda, presidential tape recordings, books, papers, and journals are kept. We want to retain that sense of historical memory in our meaning of the word archive, but we want also to include ideographs in the archives. So the archive contains not only physical and electronic material, but also the ideographs that have been inscribed on any individual personage as well as the ideographs that constitute a culture or society.

Practices are those embodied ideographs that are well established and give action its sense of appropriateness. Current practice has been authorized in the archives. We can perform research in the archives. We can reflect on current practices and question why we are doing things the way we are doing them; we can find new authority for new practices; we can reauthorize old ways. Searching the archives can also be a moment for invention, an inspiration for a new metaphor.

At every moment we consult the archives; through our habits we re-enact the archives. At any moment, we embrace democracy as we imagine it, or not. Every managerial moment carries with it the possibility that we can embrace efficiency, or not. We can enact justice, or not. We can affirm hierarchical command, or not. These values are all entwined in ideographic images, and these ideographs sometimes come into conflict at some singular moment. The moment of this impasse, this *event,*

is a time to investigate our ideographs and the relations among and between them. It is a moral and ethical moment. It might also be a time to
discover a new archive, or invent a new ideograph, or formulate a new
belief. Cassirer's (1946) understanding of symbols as producers of reality no longer seems so far fetched. Symbolic forms play a role in creating the real. The dissonances among our ideographs may claim a share
of human agency, as dissonant moments bring events to the fore from
the background. The event may be the accidental collision of ideas that
gets noticed. It may be the cogitation that gets held up to the spotlight.
The event may be the time the impasse is finally acknowledged and
confronted.

The Politics of Change

Moments of contradiction and aporia are the moments when one must
affirm liberty or equality, law or justice, a better future or lower taxes,
democracy or autocracy. Who knows what will be at stake in the next
moment of impasse? In the field of symbolization (where we find the
legacy of the archives and also the aporia of dissonance) we can look
forward to democracy—or if one prefers, efficiency, social equity, or
objectivity. Ideographic contestations are not resolvable in a programmed,
computational, statistical way. Ideographic exemplars are not derived
from some prior rule or principle.

   In cultures that have not become machines, the future does not come
to pass through social engineering. There is no transcendent morality by
which we rank-order desires. Rather, we act on a vision of democracy
(for example) but actual democracy will defer itself until the arrival of
an unknown future, an undetermined future. The archives to come are
not yet known, but their precursors are being enacted (or not) right now
in the immanence of the contingent moment.

   Holism is the view that people change their ideographic identifica-
tions in such a way as to achieve coherence with their other ideographic
attachments, to bring their beliefs and desires into some sort of symme-
try. There are no rules to follow in deciding which ideograph to down-
grade when one develops fondness for a new ideograph, or which desire
to change to accommodate a newly configured ideograph. There are no
methods for improving the way one sorts among the ideographs that
have earned pride of place in one's symbolic world. Hence, the prospects for specifying how ideographs change are not promising. It is too

holistic a process. How, then, are agreements and common understanding built?

The closest detailing we have seen as to how ideographic discourse functions in practice is Abolafia's (2004) research, drawn from transcripts of policy meetings at the U.S. Federal Reserve. He interpreted the political dynamics at a moment of a major policy change away from then-dominant monetarism, with its inclination for tight restriction of the money supply, and toward lower interest rates that would expand the money supply. A language war ensued. Abolafia's unit of analysis was the *move*, which referred to any participant's attempt to convince others, or to make a point. Framing moves were strategic actions—casting doubt, preempting an old frame, spinning a new one—to contest or maintain existing frames. From the transcripts, one could almost see the ideographs flying:

> There is a real *downturn* going on. . . . We haven't had a parallel to this situation historically except to the extent *1929* was a parallel . . . a considerable feeling in financial markets and elsewhere of developing *disarray*, a certain *floundering* . . . (355). . . . I am worried that we have gone on long enough *starving* the world economy for liquidity (363) . . . [italics added].

Abolafia attempts a categorization of the repertoire of moves, their processes, and temporal sequencing, but the process is too holistic to lend itself to thoroughgoing analytical reduction. The important point of his research for our purposes was the explicitly rhetorical struggle over practices and policies. Abolafia's *moves* are insinuations of powerful metaphors and ideographs into the conversation. The moment of impasse was (apropos the Federal Reserve) formal and far reaching in his research, but such moments can also be informal and with limited scope. Impasses, whether individual or group, are quite often the nonroutine part of the daily drill, where practices change and ideographic reality changes.

Social change occurs when the way people understand reality changes. That is, social change occurs when language changes, when categories change, when times change. As people come to understand their world differently, the sense of what is appropriate behavior (and what is not) changes; which is to say that social change happens when the ideographs transform.

Already-there ideographs, circulating among family members, neighborhood children, and the entire village are written (sometimes misspelled, sometime received differently than intended) on the still-developing personage of the child. This by-now-familiar thesis that culture is inscribed on the individual through socialization and acculturation implies that it all could have been different—and still could be.

Ideographic Transformation

Any psychic coherence that an individual or a society has achieved should be regarded as an accomplishment worth preserving—except for when a change is needed, of course. Consistent with Nietzsche's perspectivism, each of us possesses multiple perspectives on the world within ourselves. We can conjure multiple symbolizations, reflecting multiple desires, drives, fantasies, and realities. Politics—electoral and otherwise—is fought out at this level of symbolization of instincts and desires. Sentiments, too—possibly symbolized as depression or mania—compete for existence among embodied ideographs. Desire ideographs are active or passive; they empower and subvert aspirations. They become lived orientations that inhabit the subject, and they are contestable and malleable. Creed ideographs, such as the competing philosophies guiding Federal Reserve policy in the above example, supply archival context for potential transformations.

And when is change needed? There is no universal principle that can answer this question. It depends on context, which implies contingency. In any particular context, there are specific ideographs that come into play, and figuring out what to do next must be done in the context of these situational ideographs. Nor do we have a formula for determining when problem solving should begin, except that dissonance is a likely starting point. It seems to us that the impasses, the events, the moments when practices collide with other ways of doing things, when ideographs present themselves in stark contrast to other ideographs—these are the moments of possibility of incremental change to current practice.

Ideographic Events

The collision of ideographs may be personal, as when one's competence is on the line and the ideographic field becomes imbued with intensity and purpose. The impasse sparks out from a contingent set of circumstances and invokes a certain set of ideographs amidst a backdrop of cultural meaning.

At the microlevel of human affairs, we envision these impasses and events to involve the challenge or defense of local customs or personal habits.

At the macrolevel, we envision a larger role for cohering systems, such as ideology, beliefs, creed, or dogmas. At either level, status quo practices are put on the table for interrogation. Hence, politics and power relations are implicated.

From Top-Down Bureaucracy to Bottom-Up Events

In chapter 4 we described institutions as recursive practices embedded in habitual, culturally local comportments. These practices are malleable to varying degrees, but are sufficiently sedimented into daily routines as to be considered institutions. But rather than attributing organizational practices to the category *bureaucracy*, we propose to redescribe all those activities currently conceived as agencies and institutions in organizational chart boxes of the bureaucracy. Our ideographic redescription also applies to closely related sectors of civil society, such as the nonprofit social service sector and the fourth estate. As to the latter, it seems readily apparent that when satellite television and images of affluent Westerners penetrated the Iron Curtain, it became implausible for Eastern society to retain its narrow array of symbolic descriptors and stereotypes available to them before such communicative capacity existed. Though symbolic impasses can be constituted by highly local and particular norms, we also assume a public sphere with multiple sources of impasses and events.

In both philosophical and democratic theoretical terms, this is a radically pluralist vision. Ideographs in the field are influenced by the news and daily events as well as the ho-hum routines of daily practice; discussions of shared ideographic symbolizations with colleagues and compatriots can also affect the practices that are pulled from background to become figure. Conceptualizing de facto policy adjustments (recursive practices and their modifications) as vectors of momentum can highlight events and practices that current orthodoxy must, because of where that unilateralist searchlight points, leave obscure.

The Spark of Difference

An ideographic interpretation of events and impasses thus opens up avenues of interpretation unavailable to top-down, bureaucratic, command-and-control policy implementation.

An ideographic event has no real fixed physical position as naïve sender-message-receiver (S-M-R) information theory would postulate. Instead, ideography should be seen as the arena of symbolization in which a democratic pluralism of discourse formations becomes possible. This discursive approach to a hopefully democratic public administration does, we think, imply a way to subtend incommensurability and neotribalism. The symbolic meanings of particular language games may indeed grow apart and become incommensurable. But within incommensurability is the spark of difference; difference implies the collision of ideographs that can stop the action or redirect it. Following Foucault, one might be tempted to name this collision of moment of resistance, but the moment might just as easily be one of affirmation.

Our use of structuration theory and ideography implies no canon. Recursive practices can be Eurocentric, or not; male-dominated, or not; elitist or egalitarian. The recursive practices of a constitutionally founded institution are not in principle favored over the recursive practices of a central-city gang. Ideographic events and impasses can arouse sympathies and energies in many ways by many types of participants and ways of participating.

In this chapter we have laid out a new unit of analysis, the ideograph, suitable for understanding both theory and practice. Its deterministic properties are indeterminate, its reality properties abstract, its archives are rich in historical precedent and potential for new combinations. Its field of symbolization is the very field upon which politics is played and cultural contestations work themselves from background into figure.

Notes

1. Luthans and Davis (1982) used the term idiographic to argue for an interpretive approach to organizational studies that differs from nomothetic (universalizing) approaches to research. While we are proposing something consistent with this line of thinking, our ideography has a different meaning.

2. Cognitive science, Morçöl (1997) points out, separates representation from reality. Mental representations do not necessarily represent anything in that they can be pure fantasy. But mental representations also happen to be ethnocentric constructions because their raw material is mined from the images and patterns that circulate in the culture.

3. A caveat might be appropriate at this point: Not everything is equally amenable to symbolization. We happily acknowledge that ideography isn't everything. There are many sensory experiences and biological desires that escape the realm of ideography. In particular, we would suggest a possible linkage to the linguistic unconscious in that much of what is taken to be the unconscious is located there for its absence of symbolization.

4. As an examination of the posted document's properties apparently revealed, Bush's speech was authored by "feaver-p" (Shane 2005).

6

Conclusion

We started out by criticizing the overhead democratic accountability loop model for its shortcomings in claiming to advance democracy. At an ontological level, we called into question the fundaments of its reality: representation in making reality claims and representation in making democratic claims. Votes in elections these days seem uncountable —and not just in Florida in 2000, when the U.S. Supreme Court ruled that they not be recounted. In the state of Washington's gubernatorial election of 2004, the results showed that Republican Dino Rossi won by 261 votes. The automatic machine recount confirmed that Rossi had indeed won, but by only 42 votes. The Democrats requested a hand recount, and this set of results made Democrat Chris Gregoire the winner by 129 votes (Luton 2006). Senatorial and House certification ensued, as did lawsuits, and Judge John Bridges upheld the results of the third tally. Counting, like measurement in general, is not as straightforward as one might think on first blush—not in Haiti, Egypt, or the United States. It is possible that the nature of being is irreducible to the countable individual.

Majoritarian models of democracy have long been critiqued for their susceptibility to the tyranny-of-the-majority, as well as their individualistic premises. The viability of the group, not the individual, is the underlying assumption of consociational models of democracy (Lijphart 1999). In ethnically or culturally diverse societies, majoritarian models can enable dominant ethnic groups to systematically subjugate the minority group or groups (Staniševski and Miller forthcoming). Consociational democracy assigns sovereignty not to individuals aggregated into "the people," but to distinct cultural groups. Switzerland and Belgium display consociational tendencies. Consociational democracy is a form of decision making based on consensus of representatives from all cultural groups (religious, ethnic, etc.) rather than majority rule. Over-representation of minority groups as well as veto power for minority groups are part of the consociational model.

Depending on cultural context, the consociational model has advantages over majoritarian electoral models. Our objection to the consociational model is that it solidifies and reifies ethnic or religious categories. While recognition of cultural difference is an important aspect of getting along in a pluralistic world, the necessary reification of established social constructions makes redescription more difficult. In other words, to the extent that religious boundaries or ethnic identities are taken to be immutable and essential facts, the prospects of reenvisioning social practices and redescribing reality are reduced. Discursive models of democracy are more accommodating of transformational possibilities. In ideographic discourse, cultural identities are not static categories that need formal state protection, but are signifiers allowed free play in a constant process of incremental adjustment of current practice through discursive engagement.

With ontological presuppositions that are, like consociational democracy, quite different from individual unit counting protocols, ideographic discourse accommodates the student of bureaucracy who is unwilling to accept the usual categories—hierarchy, efficiency, measurement of outcomes—as incorrigible realities. In the long run, the ideograph offers a unit of analysis that respects the contingency of everyday life while offering a way of injecting coherence and human purpose into the everyday sequence of events, impasses, and habits. The ideograph organizes the chaos without reactively suppressing new expressions and desires for change. Arriving at this hopeful democratic destination comes after a long theoretical journey. A summary review is in order, ahead of some further reflection.

Orthodoxy and Its Alternatives

Deconstructing the Loop Model of Democracy

Our theorizing was eventually optimistic, but we began skeptically. Majoritarian procedural democracy theory—which begins with individual preferences that are aggregated to popular will, codified by legislation, implemented by the bureaucracy, and evaluated in turn by attentive voters—lacks credibility. This loop model not only lacks credibility as a whole process, but also none of its stages function as orthodox theory supposes they do. The attempt to realize the popular sovereignty by precisely enunciating rules to bind the behavior of governmental functionaries is misguided because of the dysfunctions of the loop; and it is undemocratic at the worksite level.

We criticized representation on parallel vectors: the empirical and the democratic. Both of them enounce a metaphysics of presence, insisting that there is some immutable, natural, and real thing we must heed: the people, the counted votes, the empirical data. It is a tight, elegant, and insuperable system—like a straightjacket. Once dressed up in one, there is no point in being for it or against it. Its metaphysics of presence tethers signifiers (or words) to terra firma, and grounds them in a foundation, rather than allowing them free play. Presence is thereby made to be the final arbiter. Omnipresent presence in the premodern days was God-the-father; in the age of science it is reality-in-itself.

In the modern social sciences, the prestige of reality-in-itself is affirmed by the oft-repeated mantra: "That is an empirical question." An election is one such empirical event. Philosophy lately (Rorty's *Philosophy and the Mirror of Nature* most particularly) casts doubt on the sort of epistemology that thinks empirical questions are that easy, that there is a one-to-one correspondence between a word and reality-in-itself. Baudrillard's now-famous cartographical map of the kingdom, which corresponds exactly to the contours of the kingdom and is exactly the same size as the kingdom, mocks the idea of one-to-one correspondence between our symbols and reality-in-itself.

But representation does not surrender easily. Citizen-voter is an empirically verifiable unit of analysis, characterized by a physical presence that can be aggregated into *the people*, which serves as the sovereign. Empirical reality and democratic accountability thus come together in a great symbolic coalescence to serve as modernity's fundamental political presupposition. This foundational presupposition serves as final arbiter. In modernity, we citizens offer ourselves up to the will of this sovereign as countable bodies and accountable citizens. We adopt a sense of purpose and efficacy befitting our democratic freedoms. We speak the language of this great sovereign and affirm its grand metaphor: the people.

But empirical individuals no longer add up to the people. The need for a final arbiter has been deconstructed as pathos, driven by a foundation-desiring Cartesian anxiety. The uneasiness with the free play of signifiers has been noted and problematized, but anxiety over loss of foundation sustains itself over the deconstruction of same. The *representative democratic accountability feedback loop* model formalizes politics and reinforces top-down authoritarianism in public administration practice. The scandal is that empirical reality and democratic rule have slipped away from their representations.

Neoliberalism: The Reform That Hates Government

Market reforms have been pressed upon public administration in the appearances of outsourcing, privatization, new public management, deregulation, and results-oriented performance measurement. We gathered these sorts of reform efforts together under the category neoliberalism. This label was chosen because of its inherent endorsement of free market principles, and also to situate the genre in political-ideological context. Nothing about public administration's free market reforms is ideologically neutral. While the neoliberal proposal has done much to undermine the orthodoxy of a neutral public administration, it also extends many of the presuppositions entailed by orthodoxy: efficiency and economy as the presumptive and unquestionable norms; science and methodological measurement protocols as normative and realizable aspirations.

Our specific criticism of these reforms had to do with their linkages to corrupt practices and their unrealizable ambitions with respect to performance assessment (which entails gaming the system by all those in subordinate roles who have few alternative strategies). In its most toxic applications, the purpose seems to disable government and render it ineffective, while distributing ill-gotten gains to corporate insiders.

Constitutionalism

Neoliberalism's discordant tone of antigovernmentalism evoked academic defense of proactive administration like that found in the Blacksburg Manifesto. This elaborate constitutional argument—the best of the lot—was an attempt to show that nonelected public servants owe allegiance first to the Constitution and only secondarily to the current incumbents of elected and politically appointed office. This argument was a well-intentioned life buoy thrown to drowning bureaucrats and a refreshing, innovative alternative to loop orthodoxy.

Despite its virtues, the Blacksburg Manifesto fell short of meeting the need for an alternative model for public administration. Neither the elected inhabitants of the loop nor the public, which has sullenly acquiesced to their rule, will be convinced by arcane constitutional scholarship. It is a weak attempt to legitimize the administrative state—including its antidemocratic tendencies toward centralization. The Blacksburg strategy entails accepting the bureau-pathologies associated with traditional, progressivist, centralized, hierarchical public administration. We judge it to be too conservative to serve as the template for liberal and discursive democracy.

Communitarianism

The maladies of loop democracy also brought forth a communitarian alternative, which interrupts the loop by directly accessing citizens. Citizen activation, civism, and similar tendencies in the public administration literature represent a serious contender to replace the orthodox model. The major strength of these efforts is that they are the manifestations in public administration of philosophical communitarianism, a view of politics that possesses a fully articulated ontology, epistemology, and cosmology rooted in ancient, medieval, and postmodern thought. Democracy, to communitarians, is not a mere procedural arrangement of dispute resolution. Citizens need to be involved in the decisions that affect their lives because it is an important aspect of communitarian teleology, of being fully human. But the communitarian ideal is too remote from current conditions to be workable. The authors of this book are communitarians in the sense of embracing many aspects of the communitarian ideal. We nonetheless assert the need for an ideographic discourse theory, in part because of our assessment of hyperreality, wherein the communitarian ideal is unlikely to be realized. The problem is not merely that civic participation consumes too many evenings and weekends, or that citizens possess "false consciousness"—although these are part of the difficulty. "The community" may not be attentive enough to solve either your public problems or ours.

Media-Infused Hyperreality

A persistent theme in this book has been the depreciating political discourse: the public policy conversation has been eclipsed by glib, insincere, attention-grabbing symbolic imagery. Tendencies in the larger culture and society should be taken into account in attempts to replace orthodoxy. Particularly salient is what we call the thinning of reality or the development of *hyperreality*. This term is used to indicate that signs and words have become increasingly estranged from democratic discourse.

Most of what passes for public conversation is not that at all. It degenerates as communication loses the check on monologue provided by open dialogue. Notable is the fatuous triviality of most claims offered in the public conversation, often an attempt to sell something. In hyperreality, words lose their capacity to signify and instead become *self-referential*, that is, meaningful only in a narrow context that is either not shared by everyone or fleeting in the sense that there is nothing beyond the moment to digest. With monologic banality dominating the media, the macroculture—taken to be the society as a whole and crossing generational, class, race, linguistic, and gender divisions—thins. Thicker, more robust, communities of discourse do develop, but only in enclaves or subcultures (a tendency referred to as *neotribalism*).

These two dialectically related tendencies—thinning macroculture and robust subcultures—make democratic will formation and policy discourse increasingly problematic. This leads, in turn, to a simulated politics wherein political entrepreneurs traffic in manipulated symbols. The fragmentation and neotribalism of hyperreality make governance of any kind difficult.

So we seek a new framework that can withstand hyperreality, on the one hand, and can claim congruence with democratic ideals, on the other. Adopting the social constructivist frame was our first move in this direction.

Constructivism and Governmentality

Recursive Practices

Theoretical presuppositions condition how things are perceived. For example, command-and-control bureaucracy would be nonsensical without the kindred assumptions of cause-and-effect determinism and the existence of rational, utility-maximizing individuals. These underlying premises and assumptions shape understandings, the propositions that stem from those understandings, and the possibilities for action that may then be imagined. We find that the underlying assumptions endemic to most public administration theorizing have led to the ongoing intellectual crisis, now decades old in public administration, a crisis that is even more poignant in conditions of hyperreality.

Mostly, too much is assumed by prevailing ontologies about the rationality of human nature, about the concreteness of organizations and institutions, about the consensus around organizational goals, and about the solidity of the key concepts and variables that shape public administration thought. We try to back away from as many of these assumptions as possible, and even go so far as to allow that reality itself is neither concrete nor objective, but constructed by humans and hence malleable.

Bureaucracy is a case in point. We often speak of "organizational goals" as if these goals were somehow separate from the goals of specific groups of humans and therefore should be privileged. Public agencies, private corporations, and bureaucratic organizations of all stripes are thought to "behave," to possess desires, and to have wants and needs just like people. The courts have gone so far as to give corporations rights of free speech and the right to influence elections, as if they were citizens. What sense can be made of these invisible institutional structures that somehow seem real? Giddens's structuration theory has helped here. He grounds institutions in social processes, a conceptualization that allows us to avoid reifying institutions, but also allows us to appreciate that there are social-structural constraints on our possibilities for action. Bureaucracy, Giddens teaches, is a structuration of repeatable practices, a conglomeration of habits, patterns of social practices that recur in rule-like fashion. Bureaucracies are but social habits and social constructions, or to use Giddens's term, *recursive practices.* This perspective on organizations—that they are social constructions rather than concrete entities—is derived also from Berger and Luckmann's (1966) *The Social Construction of Reality,* which serves as a useful reminder that we humans actively participate in creating the categories that prefigure our knowledge of the world. To avoid the unexamined reification of socially constructed categories, we shed assumption after assumption until we arrive—with Richard Rorty, Michel Foucault, and Jacques Derrida as our guides—at a space where everything is contestable and no a priori conditions or presuppositions are slipped into the meeting tent before the people get there. Rorty called this kind of place democracy.

Governmentality

Whether democratic or not, care and control of the population has been the function of government since it displaced the prince's state as the ruling regime. Public administration, in its everyday mode of operation, deploys techniques of power to extend and enforce the domain of governmental rationality. These include techniques of individualization, normalization, surveillance, and pastoralism (for example, the Employee Assistance Program); techniques of parsing the population and counting within the categories thus created; techniques of inclusion and exclusion. But these techniques of power are also exercised in domains other than public administration: in the insurance business, in the psychiatrist's office, in the stock market, in the universities that produce social science and explicate normal curves of demographic research, in nonprofit organizations.

Through techniques of *normalizaton* (examination, comparison, differentiation, correction, homogenization), *individualization* (specification of space, control of activity, and organization for forces via managerial discipline), *panopticism* (constancy of surveillance), and *pastoralism* (assurance of salvation, confession, sacrifice of power for the good of the flock), the techniques of discipline and power function to assure the subjectification of the individual as well as the governability of the population (McGinn 2006).

As Eagan (2006, 13) put it, "Foucault presents us with a less optimistic, and perhaps more accurate view of the subject . . . Foucault's subject is radically subjected to a set of circumstances that is not merely a backdrop of social meanings, but that constitute the very terms of the creation and continued existence of that subject." The point is that subjects are constructed and created through discourses—and they are not necessarily the author of their own construction. Yet despite the overwhelming power of historically informed status quo practice, the potential for resistance at the moment of impasse accompanies all expressions of power.

A Field of Political Contestation

Symbolization

The citizen-subject of governmentality is normalized, individualized, and objectified. Whatever agency remains within such a subjectified individual is highly conditioned by the ideographic array brought to bear on any contingent moment. Ideographs collide with one another at the moments of impasse on the new playing field of politics. It is not the hearts and minds, but the ideographs of culture that must be won—for the sake of ideology, creed, beliefs, theory, or any other culturally sedimented complex of ideographic symbolization. Microlevel events and impasses become moments of political contestation and purposive engagement as the ideographs at stake attract meaning and importance, directing energy toward the problematic situation. We propose the *event*, or the *impasse*, as a concept that presages the paradigmatic shift away from traditional public administration entities such as bureaucracy and organization.

The Momentous Event

Our ontological redescription takes a radical turn. Policy discourse takes place within the context of ongoing recursive practices—usually it is proposed that some social institution (set of recursive practices) be altered, adjusted, or created anew. The struggle that ensues is a struggle for meaning, in an environment in which no meanings are a priori true or ontologically fixed. Meaning is up for grabs. Politics is played out on an indeterminate field of symbolization, using ideographs.

The Changing Game

So we are not proposing a new regime of truth so much as a way of escaping such regimes, whose relentless self-validation and self-referential logic have come to colonize the cultural imagination. Thus continues the trend begun by Hobbes, who "declined the traditional vision of politics in which everything had its own prearranged position according to the Providential Order" (Pesch 2003, 52). Neoliberalism, which now owns the house of public administration, has transformed its orthodox architecture into an austere lean-to. In regular expressions of insolence toward those employed, the neoliberal masters have privatized much of the work, outsourcing everything from household management to gardening, and have purchased wholesale a garish oversupply of accountability techniques that only the do-nothing evaluation analysts have the time for.[1] The household help has been disciplined with arbitrary performance measurements that convey distrust—the usefulness of these measurements in getting the work done is speculative. Rationalism has become so irrational that it no longer functions to preserve the once-convincing façade of public administration neutrality that adorned the once-grand entrance to the estate.

Technologies of governmental rationality have been deeply implicated in the extension and insinuation of rational modalities into cultural life. Yet the commitment to rational-comprehensive implementation
of public policy leads to disappointment even among observers hoping
for successful implementation. A new game is needed. Like policymaking, policy implementation and public administration should be
viewed as processes of mutual adjustment among individuals, agencies,
interest groups, and various levels of government. The narrow billard
ball view that policy (as cause) will lead to specific measurable benefits
(effects) consistently shows failure, but the cause-effect blinders cannot
see the ambiguous policy results. These outcomes are more like the
ripples in a pond that undulate outward than a billiard stick driving a cue
ball to physics-predictable effect.

The unilateralism of the loop model leaves the field of public administration with little leeway except to appeal to higher-ups, as if the entire
government apparatus operated on billiard ball principles. Streetwise
administrators come up against the monologue of the overhead democracy loop, public administration's dysfunctional foundation. Domination and inequality in discursive communication are precisely the
indicators of democracy's absence that inspired Jürgen Habermas to theorize an arena of authentic discourse.

In his contemplation on Habermas's importance to public administration, Kelly (2004) argues that public administration's everyday moral
backdrop, instrumental rationality, lacks the communicative force that
citizen action would entail. Moral and ethical considerations, as well as
Habermasian consideration of appropriateness, should also be allowed
into the process of public discourse. Otherwise, "The state increasingly
takes up the welfare of its citizens only to find itself unable to do the job
in a way that its own citizens can find legitimate" (45). While administrative power is necessarily instrumentalist, the systematic exclusion of
communicatively generated power can and should be undermined. "If
particular administrative decisions depend exclusively on publicly in-
validated norms or arguments, then those decisions themselves are in-
valid" (Kelly 2004, 48–49).

Habermas (1996) is concerned that without the support of the
sociopolitical culture, communication adequate to practical reason will
not emerge. Even for Habermas, this needed cultural communication
does not work for the autonomous individual of majoritarian democracy. "To the extent that we become aware of the intersubjective consti-

tution of freedom, the possessive-individualist illusion of autonomy as self-ownership disintegrates. The self-assertive subject that wants to have everything at its disposal lacks an adequate relation to any tradition" (Habermas 1996, 490). It is important then, as Kelly (2004) urges, that public administration become an ally of deliberative democracy.

Molina and Spicer (2004) propose something along the same lines, only derived from Aristotelian rhetoric rather than Habermasian communication theory. They note how Aristotelian rhetorical practice might be of value because it "promotes a greater self-consciousness among administrators about their own values, encouraging them to seek ways of accommodating their values to the values of others, discourages any sense of finality in resolving value conflicts, and requires that administrators take account of the concrete specifics of particular practical situations in dealing with value conflicts" (301).

Farmer (2003, 22), too, wants public administration to pay more attention to rhetoric and the symbolic. "The symbolic is the business of all engaged in administrative and policy action," he argues. In eschewing the hydraulic rhetorical style that dominates public administration, he argues for a new group signature. "Group signatures, overlapping with individual signatures, designate the rhetorical style or habits of mind within which our group thinks and acts. He further argues that "We do speak through the vocabularies of our disciplines. We are also familiar with the idea that our discipline speaks through us; our group signature speaks through us" (23). Farmer wants the field of public administration to speak less in terms of top-down, instrumental mechanisms and efficiency protocols, and more in terms of mutuality. According to Farmer, the kind of public administration that we are is reflected in the rhetoric we deploy.

White and McSwain (1993, 33) similarly called for a semiotic approach to public administration: "Semiotic ontology tells us that our subjectivity is constituted in such a way that it is difficult if not impossible to do such a thing as make an ethical choice—especially as individuals. Our sense of self is so fragile, and our consequent need for narrative so strong that we accept the impossible moral situation into which we are put by the process of cultural signification, a situation where we are induced to feel that we must choose but can never know enough to be certain if we are choosing well." The alternative White and McSwain offer is to "band together in our terror and fragility" (33) to face together the absence of any final arbiter that will show us the path to truth.

The art of government, it seems to us, must nurture these norms of solidarity and community, but this nurturance is best performed under the influence of classical liberalism. Communities can be oppressive and cruel, if not stuck in their ways. Spicer's (2001) emphasis on value pluralism offers a welcome qualifier to communitarian conformity. But the joining of public administrators in communitarian association with citizens raises a host of other problems. Pessimistically, Alkadry (2003, following Hummel, 1994) concludes that the bureaucratic experience of technical-rational organization negatively affects the willingness of administrators to respond to citizens, giving pause to those of us who forget that long-established stable practices do not simply vanish in the light of a seemingly bright new idea. Public administrators, as objectified subjects, are both trapped in and productive of the technologies of discipline, normalization, surveillance, individualization, and pastoralism.

Happily, we have not arrived at the end of history. With Farmer and White and McSwain, we think that public administration has identified itself with a kind of ideograph, an intellectual construct, a style of talking and walking, an artifice of symbolization—and that this identification can be avoided, changed, or transformed (or reinforced, as well). While the malleability of in-place categories may be anxiety-provoking to some, the aspiration to make the administrative state a democratic state—Dwight Waldo's aspiration—can take advantage of this malleability. Indeed, today's favored practical paradigm may be tomorrow's primitivism. Policy deliberations in the public sphere may build new understandings without resort to violent uprising so long as marginalized interpretations are engaged and allowed expression. The value of tolerance (not taken as an absolute, as for example tolerance of intolerance would be self-defeating) is worth advancing among the likely values of democratic discourse.

Changing social practices in any desired direction is necessarily a communal and cultural project; our point, though, is that there is nothing foundational that public administration needs. We humans are symbol-using, culture-creating animals, trying to find ways of being together while maintaining psychic coherence in an environment of accident, chance, and decoherence. Those who practice science and rationality engage their material through symbolic exchange (White 1999). The narratives of coherence should be appreciated, but only for what they are: respectable accomplishment as coherent narrative. We count ourselves among fans of those scientists, philosophers, and scholars who are able to construct disciplined explanations, interpretations, and theories that bring understanding to the culture. Reason is not an inherent characteristic of humans or of culture, but it is a feature of some of society's best narratives. Rationality is a set of ideographs, sometimes deployed with discipline and purposive intent. One need not subscribe to any foundational conceit to be able to say that science/rationality, along with God-the-father, are among the very important cultural ideographs through which many lesser narratives are told.

Scientific ideographs, which tend to align with rational ideographs, check and limit other ideographs, including the God-the-father ideograph (which bears a genealogical resemblance to public administration's derivative hierarchy ideograph). Science-the-ideograph—entailing evolutionary biology, epidemiology, physics, clinical drug trials, and so on—has shown itself to be incredibly productive of material prosperity as well as facilitative of the health of the population—certainly when compared to the ideographies of supernaturalism. The science ideograph functions as limitation in disciplining the claims that are made in the public sphere; violating this ideograph, which has won hard-fought historical battles for influence in modern culture, is risky business. The particulars of the scientific ideograph (epistemology, methodology, norms of inquiry) can serve a valuable debunking function.

These technologies of power can also be put to use in the caring for and controlling of the population. The function of social science in modern society is to do just that, Foucault would argue. But modern technologies and their attachment to ideographs such as *progress* lose their luster in those historical moments when the earth warms, nuclear weapons proliferate, and wealth concentrates itself in the hands of a global elite.

Decoherence

The literature of public administration/policy is moving the field away from the foundational presuppositions of formal government; government is in the process of being displaced by governance (Rhodes 1997). Extra-formal political relationships (such as networks) are "displacing political parties, chief executives, and other political institutions that once served to centralize power in our fragmented governmental system" (Skok 1995, 330). However, once *bureaucracy, the executive, the party*, and *the state* are understood as reified concepts—as contingencies that are mistakenly objectified as immutable forces of nature—then the hard boundaries between and among agencies, institutions, and bureaucracies (and these distinguished from the citizenry) can be made permeable. Instead of looking at policy and administrative processes as a series of power transactions between walled institutions, think instead of a multiplicity of malleable, discursive social formations. Discursive formations such as policy communities, policy networks, interagency task forces and consortia, negotiated regulatory rulemaking, adhocracies, and the like are in abundant evidence in practice, but political and administrative scholars have only begun to build the body of theory necessary to regard these phenomena as democratic (or not).

The foundations that grounded public administration—positivist-empirical social science, pragmatism, Weberian hierarchy, scientific management, bureaucratic expertise—have become diffused due to a decohering tendency that has displaced foundationalism with a fluidity that challenges the public administration canon. Things once considered to be formal, concrete entities have become fields of play. Institutions have become sequences of recursive social practices. What were once thought to be autonomous, self-evident, and self-legitimating structures now seem more like reifications. Closed-system organizations have given way to inter-agency task forces. Objectivist, merit-based civil service now depends on *representativeness* for legitimacy. Feminist critique has redescribed public administration as systematization of masculine impulses toward control and instrumental rationality (Stivers 1993). Even citizenship is increasingly dispossessed of ties to a nation-state, as rights are distributed and claimed irrespective of nationality.

This way of concerning ourselves about public administration may be summed up as postmodernism. Social constructivism, poststructuralism, and post-Nietzschean anti-essentialist philosophy have lent their vocabularies to this new mood. The purpose of this book has been to give scholarly expression to decohering public administration in a way that opens the field toward coherent theoretical redescription. Whether such theoretical redescription should be named postmodern is an open question. *Postmodern* may be a style of thinking more than a school of thought.

Modernity is far from over, and we do not intend the term postmodern to be claiming that it is. Yet the term postmodern makes problematic important aspects of modernity. Being "for" the forms of rationality that typify public administrative practice or "against" these same forms is not a choice we are forced to accept. It is more like a contested piece of rope that rationalists and antirationalists have sunk their teeth into, at either end. Rather than join in the tug-of-war directly and endeavor to show how the rationalists (or the antirationalists) have it wrong, or that rationality is "good" or "bad," we prefer to problematize rationality as modernity's typifying mindset. Except for its arrogant overreaching, especially unwarranted in the social sciences, we are fond of it. Yet the observation that Western culture has, in no small measure, fulfilled Weber's most dire speculations about a culture-wide instrumentally rational *geist* elicits appropriate dismay. Rather than despairing, our aim has been to contribute anew to the ongoing conversation about public administration by calling forth certain aspects of the rationalistic discourse for critique. Weber painted a good portrait of modernity, but the public administration theorist "must refuse to believe this is the prettiest picture of all pictures," Waldo (1952, 100) cautioned. We deploy the term *postmodern public administration* to gather in those tendencies that would problematize the orthodox instrumental rationality that has thus far characterized public administrative practice.

In its mainstream expressions, public administration theory remains engrossed in a futile project: resuscitating the remnants of progressivism. Postmodern thought (with its perspectivism and antifoundationalism) offers something different: a new kind of fiber through which the fabric of public administration may be rewoven, and a new language through which it can be redescribed. Does public administration need to be redescribed along the lines suggested in this book? We think so. An all-too-familiar stereotype depicts public administrators as empty vessels, as sieves, as obsequious servants of the powerful interests that control the institutions of government. Such a public administrator accepts the current power arrangements as an expression of the modern sovereign, which is to say, the people. Quite often, public administrators, in their assertive quiescence, reinforce this stereotype. Their utterances are the words of people who know and enjoy the assurance that attends the insider. They can feel comfort in the knowledge that their view of the world comports well with that of the mighty apparatus of government. This culture of conformance also produces a threat: a bureaucratic takeover of the institutions of government. Hence, the usual images available for the public administrator oscillate between obsequious toady and powerful technician. Perhaps a new story line would produce new images.

In this book we have sought to put forth a different image of politics, sovereignty, and public administration. To do so requires that we extract the exhausted concepts of sovereignty, the people, and public adminis- tration from their essentialist presuppositions. We have sought to redi- rect thinking about public policy and administration in light of the irrationalities brought into practice by rationalistic processes. This redi- rection requires a kit bag of conceptual tools, some new, some borrowed, and some reforged for the task at hand. The tools have been engineered to break down that aging rusted machine and the institutional parts of which it is composed. Once we recognize that contingent human prac- tices are mistakenly objectified as immutable forces of nature, then the hard boundaries—between and among agencies, institutions, and bu- reaucracy, and these distinguished from the citizenry—can be made per- meable. Social practices are malleable and hence changeable.

Implications

In the era of results and outcomes, public administrators feel obliged to submit bogus performance results. The fakery, the deceit, the smarmy half-truths, and the enforced regimen of silence upon knowing public administrators—these official measures debase us all, especially when they succeed. Whether they are scientists at NASA with something to say about global warming who are forced instead to insert mealy-mouthed material into their public reports, or contract oversight officers with some- thing to say about graft-laden service-procurement contracts, or whistle- blowers who risk everything to bust corrupt higher-ups, the discursive public administration that we have been advocating demands that their voices be heard. O'Leary (2005) places "guerrillas in government" at the locus of the conflict between bureaucracy and democracy and at the very point of what we have called an ideographic event. As O'Leary put it, "There is a need for accountability and control in our government organizations, but that same accountability and control can stifle inno- vation and positive change. Put another way, there is a need in govern- ment for career bureaucrats who are policy innovators and risk takers; at the same time there is a need in government for career bureaucrats who are policy sustainers" (100). Either way, for sustainer or innovator, the ethical conflicts inherent in obedient practice frequently generate an impasse that practitioners cannot simply ignore.

We have understood public administration to be thoroughly drenched in politics. Its practices were put into place by the political victors; reforms of those practices are political moments, and the cordoning-off of administration from politics is but a (convenient and sometimes successful) strategy in service of a political purpose. The techniques of public administration are techniques of power, aimed at the care and control of the population.

Public administration is situated in its cultural context and contributes in important ways in shaping that same culture. Hyperreality enables sloganeering policy formulation based on cute-sounding policy prescriptions such as "three strikes and you're out"—another marijuana smoker gets stuffed into a prison cell. Before you know it, corrections facilities are bursting at the seams and public administrators are called in to sew patches. Symbolization is a cultural process, and ideographs are cultural products. They have material effects. As full-fledged participants in the technologies of care and control, public administrators adjust practices, contribute to the discourse, and attempt to resolve impasses and dissonance—along with everyone else who pays attention and seeks to make things better.

Note

1. Cunningham and Weschler (2002) made the interesting assessment that most of mainstream public administration journal articles, especially data-driven analyses, would be more useful to staff analysts than to line managers. As they put it: "The postmodernist is the natural ally of the line manager. Postmodernists reflect theories in use from a variety of perspectives and privilege no orthodoxy. Appreciating diverse perspectives provides the information base that a line manager needs to formulate effective policy or implementation strategy" (108).

References

Abolafia, Mitchel Y. 2004. "Framing Moves: Interpretive Politics at the Federal Reserve." *Journal of Public Administration Research and Theory* 14(3): 349–70.

Adams, Guy B., Priscilla V. Bowerman, Kenneth M. Dolbeare, and Camilla Stivers. 1990. "Joining Purpose to Practice: A Democratic Identity for the Public Service." In *Images and Identities in Public Administration,* eds. Henry D. Kass and Bayard L. Catron, 219–40. Newbury Park, CA: Sage Publications.

Alkadry, Mohamad. 2003. "Deliberative Discourse Between Citizens and Administrators: If Citizens Talk Will Administrators Listen?" *Administration & Society* 35(2): 184–209.

Arenson, Karen W. 2006. "Officials Say Scoring Errors for SAT Were Understated." *New York Times,* March 9, A14.

Bachrach, Peter. 1967. *The Theory of Democratic Elitism.* Boston: Little, Brown.

Barber, Benjamin R. 1984. *Strong Democracy: Participatory Politics for a New Age.* Berkeley: University of California Press.

———. 2004. *A Place for Us: How to Make Society Civil and Democracy Strong.* New York: Hill and Wang.

Barstow, David, and Robin Stein. 2005. "Under Bush, a New Age of Prepackaged News." *New York Times,* March 13, A1ff.

Barthes, Roland. 1977. *Elements of Semiology.* Trans. Annette Lavers and Colin Smith. New York: Hill and Wang.

———. 1978. "The Photographic Image." In Roland Barthes, *Image-Music-Text,* Trans. and ed. Stephen Heath, 15–31. New York: Noonday Press.

Barzelay, Michael. 2001. *The New Public Management: Improving Research and Policy Dialogue.* Berkeley: University of California Press.

Baudrillard, Jean. 1981. *For a Critique of the Political Economy of the Sign.* Trans. C. Levin. St. Louis, MO: Telos Press.

———. 1983. *Simulations.* New York: Semiotext(e).

Beiner, Ronald. 1983. *Political Judgment.* Chicago: University of Chicago Press.

Bellah, Robert N., Richard Madsen, William M. Sullivan, Ann Swidler, and Steven M. Tipton. 1985. *Habits of the Heart: Individualism and Commitment in American Life.* Berkeley: University of California Press.

———. 1991. *The Good Society.* New York: Knopf.

Bennett, W. Lance. 1998. "The UnCivic Culture: Communication, Identity, and the Rise of Lifestyle Politics." *PS: Political Science and Politics* 31(4): 740–61.

Beresford, Annette. 2000. "Simulated Budgeting." *Administrative Theory & Praxis* 22(3): 479–97.

Berger, Peter L., and Thomas Luckmann. 1966. *The Social Construction of Reality: A Treatise in the Sociology of Knowledge.* Garden City, NY: Doubleday.

Bergquist, William H. 1993. *The Postmodern Organization: Mastering the Art of Irreversible Change.* San Francisco, CA: Jossey-Bass.

Berlin, Isaiah. 1969. *Four Essays on Liberty.* New York: Oxford University Press.

———. 1979. *Concepts and Categories: Philosophical Essays.* Ed. H. Hardy. New York: Viking Press.

Bernstein, Richard J. 1992. *The New Constellation: The Ethical-Political Horizons of Modernity/Postmodernity.* Cambridge: MIT Press.

Blumenthal, Sidney. 1980. *The Permanent Campaign: Inside the World of Elite Political Operatives.* Boston: Beacon Press.

Botwinick, Aryeh. 1993. *Postmodernism and Democratic Theory.* Philadelphia, PA: Temple University Press.

Box, Richard C. 1998. *Citizen Governance: Leading American Communities into the 21st Century.* Thousand Oaks, CA: Sage Publications.

———. 1999. "Running Government like a Business: Implications for Public Administration Theory and Practice." *American Review of Public Administration* 29(1): 19–43.

Buchanan, James H., and Gordon Tullock. 1962. *The Calculus of Consent: Logical Foundations of Constitutional Democracy.* Ann Arbor: University of Michigan Press.

Burke, John P. 1986. *Bureaucratic Responsibility.* Baltimore, MD: Johns Hopkins University Press.

Burnier, DeLysa. 2005. "Making It Meaning Full: *Postmodern Public Administration* and Symbolic Interactionism." *Administrative Theory & Praxis* 27(3): 498–516.

Calinescu, Matei. 1991. "From the One to the Many: Pluralism in Today's Thought." In *Zeitgeist in Babel: The Postmodernist Controversy,* ed. Ingeborg Hoesterey, 156–74. Bloomington: Indiana University Press.

Cassirer, Ernst. 1946. *Language and Myth.* New York: Dover Publications.

Catlaw, Thomas J. 2005. "Constitution as Executive Order: The Administrative State and the Political Ontology of 'We the People.'" *Administration & Society* 37(4): 445–82.

———. Forthcoming. *The Biopolitical State, Public Administration and the Fabrication of the People.* Tuscaloosa: University of Alabama Press.

Chandler, Ralph C. 1984. "The Public Administrator as Representative Citizen: A New Role for the New Century." *Public Administration Review* 44: 196–206.

Cochran, Clarke E. 1982. *Character, Community and Politics.* Tuscaloosa: University of Alabama Press.

Cooper, Philip J. 1990. Appendix: Selected Responses. In Wamsley et al., *Refounding Public Administration,* 311–13. Newbury Park, CA: Sage.

Cooper, Terry L. 1987. "Hierarchy, Virtue, and the Practice of Public Administration: A Perspective for Normative Ethics." *Public Administration Review* 47: 320–28.

———. 1991. *An Ethic of Citizenship for Public Administration.* Englewood Cliffs, NJ: Prentice-Hall.

Courty, Pascal, and Gerald Marschke. 2003. "Dynamics of Performance-Measurement Systems." *Oxford Review of Economic Policy* 19: 268–84.

Crick, Francis. 1994. *The Astonishing Hypothesis: The Scientific Search for the Soul.* New York: Scribner's.

Cunningham, Robert, and Louis Weschler. 2002. "Theory and the Public Administration Student/Practitioner." *Public Administration Review* 62(1): 104–11.

Czarniawska, Barbara. 1997. "Symbolism in Public Administration Organization Studies." *Administrative Theory & Praxis* 19(2): 154–70.

Dahl, Robert. 1971. *Polyarchy: Participation and Opposition.* New Haven, CT: Yale University Press.

DeHaven-Smith, Lance, and Kenneth C. Jenne II. 2006. "Management by Inquiry: A Discursive Accountability System for Large Organizations." *Public Administration Review* 65(1): 64–76.

D'Entreves, Maurizio P. 1992. "Communitarianism." In *Encyclopedia of Ethics,* vol. 1, eds. Lawrence C. Becker and Charlotte B. Becker, 181–85. New York: Garland.

Derrida, Jacques. 1973. *Speech and Phenomena.* Evanston, IL: Northwestern University Press.

———. 1976. *Of Grammatology.* Trans. Gayatri Chakravorty Spivak. Baltimore, MD: Johns Hopkins University Press.

———. 1980a. "Freud and the Scene of Writing." In *Writing and Difference,* trans. Alan Bass, 196–231. Chicago: University of Chicago Press.

———. 1980b. *Writing and Difference.* Trans. Alan Bass. Chicago: University of Chicago Press.

———. 1991 (originally published in 1981). "The Double Session." Reprinted in *A Derrida Reader: Between the Blinds,* ed. Peggy Kamuf, 171–99. New York: Columbia University Press.

Dewey, John. 1997. "The Influence of Darwinism on Philosophy." In *The Influence of Darwin on Philosophy and Other Essays.* 1–19, Amherst, NY: Prometheus Books. Essay cited was originally published in 1909.

Duverger, Maurice. 1954. *Political Parties, Their Organization and Activity in the Modern State.* New York: John Wiley.

Eagan, Jennifer L. 2006. "The De-formation of Decentered Subjects: Foucault and Postmodern Public Administration." Paper presented at the conference of the Public Administration Theory Network, Olympia, WA, February 9–10.

Eckholm, Erik. 2005a. "Army Contract Official Critical of Halliburton Pact Is Demoted." *New York Times,* August 29, A9.

———. 2005b. "Halliburton Case Is Referred to Justice Dept., Senator Says." *New York Times,* November 19, A8.

Eco, Umberto. 1985. "How Culture Conditions the Colours We See." In *On Signs: A Semiotics Reader,* ed. Marshall Blonsky, 157–75. Oxford: Basil Blackwell. Reprinted in *The Communication Theory Reader*, ed. Paul Cobley, 148–71. London: Routledge, 1996.

Edelman, Murray. 1964. *The Symbolic Uses of Politics.* Urbana: University of Illinois Press.

———. 1971. *Politics as Symbolic Action.* New York: Academic Press.

———. 1977. *Political Language: Words that Succeed and Policies that Fail.* New York: Academic Press.

————. 1988. *Constructing the Political Spectacle.* Chicago: University of Chicago Press.

Eubanks, Cecil L., and Peter A. Petrakis. 1999. "Reconstructing the World: Albert Camus and the Symbolization of Experience." *Journal of Politics* 61(2): 293–312.

Farmer, David John. 1995. *The Language of Public Administration: Bureaucracy, Modernity, and Postmodernity.* Tuscaloosa: University of Alabama Press.

————. 2003. "The Allure of Rhetoric and the Truancy of Poetry." *Administrative Theory & Praxis* 25(1): 9–36.

————. 2005. *To Kill the King: Post-Traditional Governance and Bureaucracy.* Armonk, NY: M.E. Sharpe.

Finer, Herman. 1940. "Administrative Responsibility in Democratic Government." In *Public Policy,* ed. Carl Friedrich, 247–75. Cambridge: Harvard University Press.

Flyvbjerg, Bent. 2001. *Making Social Science Matter: Why Social Inquiry Fails and How It Can Succeed Again.* Cambridge: Cambridge University Press.

Foucault, Michel. 1970. *The Order of Things: An Archaeology of Human Sciences.* New York: Random House.

————. 1972. *The Archaeology of Knowledge & the Discourse on Language.* Trans. A. M. Sheridan Smith. New York: Pantheon Books.

————. 1977. *Discipline and Punish: The Birth of the Prison.* New York: Pantheon.

————. 1979. "Governmentality." Trans. Pasquale Pasquino. *Ideology and Consciousness* 6 (Autumn): 5–21.

————. 1984a. "What Is Enlightenment?" In *The Foucault Reader,* ed. Paul Rabinow, 32–50. New York: Pantheon Books.

————. 1984b. "Truth and Power." In *The Foucault Reader,* ed. Paul Rabinow, 51–75. New York: Pantheon Books.

————. 1994a. "So Is It Important to Think?" In *Michel Foucault: Power*, ed. James D. Faubion. Trans. Robert Hurley et al., 454–58. New York: The New Press.

————. 1994b. "The Birth of Biopolitics." In *Ethics: Subjectivity and Truth.* Ed. Paul Rabinow. Trans. Robert Hurley et al., 73–79. New York: The New Press.

————. 1994c. "The Political Technology of Individuals." In *Michel Foucault: Power,* ed. James D. Faubion. Trans. Robert Hurley et al., 403–17. New York: The New Press.

————. 1994d. "The Subject and Power." In *Michel Foucault: Power,* ed. James D. Faubion. Trans. Robert Hurley et al., 326–48. New York: The New Press.

Fox, Charles J. 1993. "The Use of Philosophy in Public Administration Ethics." In *Handbook on Administrative Ethics,* ed. Terry L. Cooper, 83–106. New York: Marcel Dekker.

Fox, Charles J., and Clarke E. Cochran. 1990. "Discretionary Public Administration: Toward a Platonic Guardian Class?" In *Images and Identities in Public Administration,* eds. Henry D. Kass and Bayard L. Catron, 87–112. Newbury Park, CA: Sage Publications.

Fox, Charles J., and Hugh T. Miller. 1993. "Postmodern Public Administration: A Short Treatise on Self-Referential Epiphenomena." *Administrative Theory & Praxis* 15(1): 1–17.

————. 1995. *Postmodern Public Administration: Toward Discourse.* Thousand Oaks, CA: Sage.

Frederickson, H. George. 1982. "The Recovery of Civism in Public Administration." *Public Administration Review* 42: 501–08.

Friedrich, Carl. 1940. "Public Policy and the Nature of Administrative Responsibility." In *Public Policy,* ed. Carl Friedrich, 221–45.Cambridge: Harvard University Press.

Frissen, P.H.A. 1999. *Politics, Governance and Technology: A Postmodern Narrative on the Virtual State.* Cheltenham, UK: Edward Elgar.

Fritschler, A. Lee. 1975. *Smoking and Politics: Policymaking and the Federal Bureaucracy.* 2nd ed. New York: Prentice-Hall.

Gawthrop, Louis C. 1984. "Civis, Civitas and Civilitas: A New Focus for the Year 2000." *Public Administration Review.* 34: 101–07.

Gerth, H.H., and C. Wright Mills, trans. and eds. 1946. *From Max Weber: Essays in Sociology.* New York: Oxford University Press.

Gherardi, Silvia. 1999. "A Symbolic Approach to Competence Development." *Human Resource Development International* 2(4): 313–34.

Giddens, Anthony. 1984. *The Constitution of Society: Outline of the Theory of Structuration.* Berkeley: University of California Press.

———. 1990. *The Consequences of Modernity.* Palo Alto, CA: Stanford University Press.

Greenhouse, Linda. 2005. "Justices Reject F.B.I. Translator's Appeal on Termination." *New York Times,* November 29, A22.

Habermas, Jürgen. 1972. *Knowledge and Human Interests.* Trans. J.J. Shapiro. Boston: Beacon Press.

———. 1996. *Between Facts and Norms: Contributions to a Discourse Theory of Law and Democracy.* Trans.William Rehg. Cambridge: MIT Press.

Hardin, Garrett. 1968. "The Tragedy of the Commons." *Science* 162: 1243–48.

Hatch, Mary Jo. 1997. *Organization Theory: Modern, Symbolic, and Postmodern Perspectives.* New York: Oxford University Press.

Hawking, Stephen. 1988. *A Brief History of Time.* New York: Bantam.

Hirsh, Arthur. 1981. *The French New Left: An Intellectual History from Sartre to Gorz.* Boston: South End Press.

Hofstadter, Douglas R. 1999. *Gödel, Escher, Bach: An Eternal Golden Braid.* New York: Basic Books.

Horn, Murray J. 1995. *The Political Economy of Public Administration: Institutional Choice in the Public Sector.* New York: Cambridge University Press.

Howe, Louis. 2001. "Civil Service Reform and the Political Culture of Governmentality: Massachusetts 1952–1981." *Administrative Theory & Praxis* 23(2): 151–74.

Hummel, Ralph P. 1994. *The Bureaucratic Experience: A Critique of Life in the Modern Organization.* New York: St. Martin's Press.

Imas, J.M. 2005. "Rational Darkness: Voicing the Unheard in the Modern Management Discourse of Chile." *Administrative Theory & Praxis* 27(1): 111–33.

Jahn, Robert G., and Brenda J. Dunne. 1986. "On the Quantum Mechanics of Consciousness, with Application to Anomalous Phenomena." *Foundations of Physics* 16(8): 721–72.

Jameson, Fredric. 1991. *Postmodernism or the Cultural Logic of Late Capitalism.* Durham, NC: Duke University Press.

Janosik, Robert. J. 1987. *Encyclopedia of the American Judicial System: Studies of the Principal Institutions and Processes of Law.* New York: Scribner's.

Jonsen, Albert R., and Stephen S. Toulmin. 1988. *The Abuse of Casuistry: A History of Moral Reasoning.* Berkeley: University of California Press.

Kauffman, Matthew. 2005. "Charities Shortchange Veterans in Relation to Dona-
tions." *Hartford Courant.* Reprinted in *South Florida Sun-Sentinel,* November
10, 12A.
Kellner, Douglas. 1989. *Jean Baudrillard: From Marxism to Postmodernism and
Beyond.* Palo Alto, CA: Stanford University Press.
Kelly, Terrence. 2004. "Unlocking the Iron Cage: Public Administration in the De-
liberative Democratic Theory of Jürgen Habermas." *Administration & Society*
36(1): 38–61.
Kettl, Donald F. 1997. "The Global Revolution in Public Management: Driving
Themes, Missing Links." *Journal of Policy Analysis and Management.* 16(3):
446–62.
King, Cheryl Simrell, and Camilla Stivers et al. 1998. *Government Is Us: Public Ad-
ministration in an Anti-Government Era.* Thousand Oaks, CA: Sage Publications.
Kleindienst, Linda. 2006. "State to Hire Temps to Grade the FCAT." *South Florida
Sun-Sentinel,* March 9, 1Bff.
Kronenberg, Phil S. 1990. "Public Administration and the Defense Department:
Examination of a Prototype." In *Refounding Public Administration,* eds. Gary L.
Wamsley et al., 274–306. Newbury Park, CA: Sage Publications.
Krugman, Paul. 2005. "A Private Obsession." *New York Times,* November 18, A27.
Kuhn, Thomas. 1970. *The Structure of Scientific Revolutions.* 2nd ed. Chicago:
University of Chicago Press.
Lakoff, George. 2002. *Moral Politics: How Liberals and Conservatives Think.* 2nd
ed. Chicago: University of Chicago Press.
———. 2004. *Don't Think of an Elephant: Know Your Values and Frame the De-
bate.* White River Junction, VT: Chelsea Green Publishing.
Lakoff, George, and Mark Johnson. 1980. *Metaphors We Live By.* Chicago: Univer-
sity of Chicago Press.
Lenoir, Timothy. 1994. "Was That Last Turn a Right Turn?: The Semiotic Turn and
A.J. Greimas." *Configurations* 2: 119–36.
Lijphart, Arend. 1999. *Patterns of Democracy: Government Forms and Performance
in Thirty-Six Countries.* New Haven, CT: Yale University Press.
Lindahl, Hans. 1998. "Democracy and the Symbolic Constitution of Society." *Ratio
Juris* 11(1): 12–37.
Lindblom, Charles E. 1977. *Politics and Markets: The World's Political-Economic
Systems.* New York: Basic Books.
———. 2001. *The Market System: What It Is, How It Works, and What to Make of
It.* New Haven, CT: Yale University Press.
Lipsky, Michael. 1980. *Street-Level Bureaucracy: Dilemmas of the Individual in
Public Services.* New York: Russell Sage.
Lowi, Theodore J. 1964. "American Business, Public Policy, Case-Studies, and Po-
litical Theory." *World Politics* 16(4): 677–715.
———. 1969. *The End of Liberalism: Ideology, Policy and the Crisis of Public
Authority.* New York: W.W. Norton.
———. 1993. "Legitimizing Public Administration: A Disturbed Dissent." *Public
Administration Review* 53(3): 261–64.
Luthans, Fred, and Tim R.V. Davis. 1982. "An Idiographic Approach to Organiza-
tional Behavior Research: The Use of Single Case Experimental Designs and
Direct Measures." *Academy of Management Review* 7(3): 380–91.

Luton, Larry. 2006. "Connoting 'Empirical': Imports for Public Administration." Paper presented at the Public Administration Theory Network Conference, Olympia, Washington, February 9–10.

Lynn, Laurence. 1996. *Public Management as Art, Science, and Profession.* Chatham, NJ: Chatham House Publishers.

Lyotard, Jean-Francois. 1984. *The Postmodern Condition: A Report on Knowledge.* Trans. G. Bennington and B. Massumi. Minneapolis: University of Minnesota Press.

MacIntyre, Alasdair. 1984. *After Virtue: A Study in Moral Theory.* 2nd ed. Notre Dame, IN: Notre Dame University Press.

Marcuse, Herbert. 1964. *One Dimensional Man: Studies in the Ideology of Advanced Industrial Society.* Boston: Beacon Press.

McConnell, Grant. 1966. *Private Power and American Democracy.* New York: Knopf.

McGee, Michael Calvin. 1980. "The 'Ideograph': A Link Between Rhetoric and Ideology." *Quarterly Journal of Speech* 66: 1–16. Reprinted in Carl R. Burgchart, *Readings in Rhetorical Criticism,* 2nd ed. State College, PA: Strata Publishing, 2000, 456–70.

McGinn, Kathleen A. 2006. "Relationships of Power and Resistance in Street Level Organizations." Doctoral dissertation, Florida Atlantic University.

McMahon, Paula. 2006. "First Misconduct Trial Starts." *South Florida Sun-Sentinel,* February 16, 1B ff.

McSwite, O.C. 1997. *Legitimacy in Public Administration: A Discourse Analysis.* Newbury Park, CA: Sage Publications.

———. 2002. *An Invitation to Public Administration.* Armonk: NY: M.E. Sharpe.

Mead, George H. 1967. *Mind, Self, and Society: From the Standpoint of a Social Behaviorist.* Chicago: University of Chicago Press.

Miller, Hugh T. 2002. *Postmodern Public Policy.* Albany, NY: SUNY Press.

Miller, Hugh T., and James R. Simmons. 1998. "The Irony of Privatization." *Administration & Society* 30(5): 513–32.

Molina, Anthony Deforest, and Michael W. Spicer. 2004. "Aristotelian Rhetoric, Pluralism, and Public Administration." *Administration & Society* 36(3): 282–305.

Morçöl, Göktug. 1997. "The Epistemic Necessity of Using Metaphors in Organizational Theory: A Constructivist Argument. *Administrative Theory and Praxis.* 19(1): 43–57.

———. 2002. *A New Mind for Policy Analysis: Toward a Post-Newtonian and Postpositivist Epistemology and Methodology.* Westport, CT: Praeger.

Morgan, Douglas F. 1990. "Administrative Phronesis: Discretion and the Problem of Administrative Legitimacy in Our Constitutional System." In *Images and Identities in Public Administration,* eds. Henry D. Kass and Bayard L. Catron, 67–86. Newbury Park, CA: Sage Publications.

Morgan, David R., and Robert E. England. 1988. "The Two Faces of Privatization." *Public Administration Review* 48(6): 979–87.

Morgan, Gareth. 1986. *Images of Organization.* Newbury Park, CA: Sage Publications.

Mosca, Gaetano. 1939. *The Ruling Class.* Trans. Hannah D. Kahn, ed. Arthur Livingston. New York: McGraw-Hill.

Mosher, Frederick C. 1982. *Democracy and the Public Service.* 2nd ed. New York: Oxford University Press.

National Science Foundation. 2005. "Synopsis." Available at www.nsf.gov/funding/pgm_summ.jsp?pims_id=5418&org=SES&from=home. Accessed May 23, 2006.

Nietzsche, Friedrich. 1885, reprinted 1992. *Beyond Good and Evil.* In *Basic Writings of Nietzsche.* Trans. Walter Kaufmann, 179–434. New York: The Modern Library.

———. 1887, reprinted 1992. *Genealogy of Morals.* In *Basic Writings of Nietzsche.* Trans. Walter Kaufmann, 437–599. New York: The Modern Library.

———. 1974. *The Gay Science: With a Prelude in Rhymes and an Appendix of Songs.* Trans. Walter Kaufmann. New York: Random House/Vintage Books. Originally published in 1887 as the second edition of *Die Fröhliche Wissenschaft.*

Oakeshott, Michael. 1991. *Rationalism in Politics and Other Essays.* Indianapolis, IN: Liberty Press.

O'Leary, Rosemary. 2005. *The Ethics of Dissent: Managing Guerilla Government.* Washington, DC: CQ Press.

Overman, E.S. 1991. "Policy Physics." In *Quantum Politics: Applying Quantum Theory to Political Phenomena,* ed. Theodore L. Becker, 151–67. New York: Praeger.

Page, Benjamin I., and Richard A. Brody. 1972. "Policy Voting and the Electoral Process." *American Political Science Review* 66: 979–95.

Pateman, Carole. 1970. *Participation and Democratic Theory.* London: Cambridge University Press.

Pesch, Udo. 2003. "Exploring the Public/Private Dichotomy: An Evaluation of 'The Intellectual Crisis of American Public Administration' and 'The Government is Us'." In Mark R. Rutgers, ed., *Retracing Public Administration,* 37–75. Oxford: Elsevier.

Pollin, Robert. 2005. *Contours of Descent: U.S. Economic Fractures and the Landscape of Global Austerity.* London: Verso.

Popper, Karl R. 1959. *The Logic of Scientific Discovery.* New York: Basic Books.

Poster, Mark. 1990. *The Mode of Information: Poststructuralism and Social Context.* Chicago: University of Chicago Press.

Prewitt, Kenneth. 1970. "Political Ambitions, Volunteerism, and Electoral Accountability." *American Political Science Review* 64: 5–17.

Rabinow, Paul, ed. 1984. *The Foucault Reader.* New York: Pantheon.

Rhodes, R.A.W. 1997. *Understanding Governance: Policy Networks, Governance, Reflexivity and Accountability.* Philadelphia, PA: Open University Press.

Riccucci, Norma. 2005. "Street-Level Bureaucrats and Intrastate Variation in the Implementation of Temporary Assistance for Needy Families Policies." *Journal of Public Administration Research and Theory* 15(1): 89–111.

Roe, Emery M. 1994. *Narrative Policy Analysis: Theory and Practice.* Durham, NC: Duke University Press.

Rohr, John. 1986. *To Run a Constitution: The Legitimacy of the Administrative State.* Lawrence: University Press of Kansas.

———. 1989. *Ethics for Bureaucrats: An Essay on Law and Values.* 2nd ed. New York: Marcel Dekker.

———. 1993. "Toward a More Perfect Union." *Public Administration Review* 53(3): 273–74.

Rorty, Richard. 1979. *Philosophy and the Mirror of Nature.* Princeton, NJ: Princeton University Press.

————. 1991. *Essays on Heidegger and Others.* Philosophical papers. Vol. 2. Cambridge: Cambridge University Press.

————. 1999. "An Appreciation of Jacques Derrida." *Stanford [online] Report,* April 21. Available at http://news-service.stanford.edu/news/1999/april21/rortytext-421.html. Accessed May 23, 2006.

Rosenbloom, David H. 2000. *Building a Legislative-Centered Public Administration: Congress and the Administrative State, 1946–1999.* Tuscaloosa: University of Alabama Press.

Sandel, Michael J. 1996. *Democracy's Discontent: America in Search of a Public Philosophy.* Cambridge, MA: Belknap Press.

Schattschneider, E. E. 1960. *The Semnisovereign People: A Realist's View of Democracy in America.* New York: Holt, Rinehart and Winston.

Schmitt, Eric. 2005. "Propaganda: Military Admits Planting News in Iraq." *New York Times,* December 3, A11.

Schutz, Alfred. 1955. "Symbol, Reality, and Society." In *Symbols and Society: Fourteenth Symposium,* eds. Lyman Bryson et al., 282–329. New York: Harper.

Shane, Scott. 2005. "Bush's Speech on Iraq War Echoes Voice of an Analyst." *New York Times,* December 4, A1.

Shenon, Philip. 2005. "Demotion of a Prosecutor Is Investigated." *New York Times,* September 27, A21.

Skok, J. E. 1995. "Policy Issue Networks and the Public Policy Cycle: A Structural-Functional Framework for Public Administration. *Public Administration Review* 55(4): 323–32.

"Soldiers Told to Intervene in Abuse." 2005. *New York Times,* November 30, A10.

Spicer, Michael. 2001. *Public Administration and the State: A Postmodern Perspective.* Tuscaloosa: University of Alabama Press.

————. 2003. "Masks of Freedom: An Examination of Isaiah Berlin's Ideas on Freedom and Their Implications for Public Administration." *Administrative Theory & Praxis* 25(4): 545–88.

Spicer, Michael, and Larry D. Terry. 1993. "Legitimacy, History, and Logic: Public Administration and the Constitution." *Public Administration Review* 53(3): 239–46.

Staniševski, Dragan, and Hugh T. Miller. Forthcoming. "Deliberative Public Administration: The Discourse Alternative." In *Public Administration in Transition,* eds. Gunnar Gjelstrup and Eva Sørensen. Copenhagen: DJØF Publishing and McGill-Queens University Press.

Stivers, Camilla. 1990. "Active Citizenship and Public Administration." In *Refounding Public Administration,* eds. Gary L. Wamsley et al., 246–73. Newbury Park, CA: Sage Publications.

————. 1993. *Gender Images in Public Administration: Legitimacy and the Administrative State.* Newbury Park, CA: Sage.

Stone, Deborah A. 1988. *Policy Paradox and Political Reason.* Glenview, IL: Scott Foresman/Little, Brown.

Sundquist, James L. 1973. *Dynamics of the Party System: Alignment and Realignment of Political Parties in the United States.* Washington, DC: Brookings Institution Press.

Taylor, Charles. 1985. *Philosophical Papers,* 2 vols. New York: Cambridge University Press.

Thompson, Fred. 2003. "Why a New Public Management? Why Now?" *Review of Public Personnel Administration* 23(4): 328–35.

Townley, Barbara, David J. Cooper, and Leslie Oakes. 2003. "Performance Measures and the Rationalization of Organizations." *Organization Studies* 24(7): 1045–72.

U.S. Office of Management and Budget. 2003. "Performance Measurement Challenges and Strategies." June 18. Available at www.whitehouse.gov/omb/part/challenges_strategies.pdf. Accessed May 23, 2006.

Voegelin, Eric. 1952. *The New Science of Politics.* Chicago: University of Chicago Press.

Waldo, Dwight. 1948, reprinted 2006. *The Administrative State: A Study of the Political Theory of American Public Administration.* Somerset, NJ: Transaction Publishers.

———. 1952. "Development of Theory of Democratic Administration." *American Political Science Review* 46(1): 81–103.

———. 1984. *The Administrative State: A Study of the Political Theory of American Public Administration,* 2nd ed. London: Holmes and Meier.

Wallace, B. Alan. 1989. *Choosing Reality: A Contemplative View of Physics and the Mind.* Boston: New Science Library.

Walzer, Michael. 1970. *Obligations: Essays on Disobedience, War and Citizenship.* Cambridge: Harvard University Press.

———. 1983. *Spheres of Justice.* New York: Basic Books.

Wamsley, Gary L. 1990. "Introduction." In *Refounding Public Administration,* 19–29.

Wamsley, Gary L., Robert N. Bacher, Charles T. Goodsell, Philip S. Kronenberg, John A. Rohr, Camilla M. Stivers, Orion F. White, and James F. Wolf, eds. 1990. *Refounding Public Administration.* Newbury Park, CA: Sage.

Weber, Max. 1946. *From Max Weber: Essays in Sociology.* Ed. and trans. H. H. Gerth and C. W. Mills. New York: Oxford University Press.

White, Jay D. 1999. *Taking Language Seriously: The Narrative Foundations of Public Administration Research.* Washington, DC: Georgetown University Press.

White, Leonard D. 1958. *The Republican Era: 1869–1901.* New York: The Macmillan Company.

White, Orion F., and Cynthia J. McSwain. 1993. "The Semiotic Way of Knowing and Public Administration." *Administrative Theory & Praxis* 15(1): 18–35.

Wittgenstein, Ludwig. 1953. *Philosophical Investigations.* New York: Macmillan.

Yanow, Dvora. 2002. *Constructing Race and Ethnicity in America: Category-Making in Public Policy and Administration.* Armonk, NY: M.E. Sharpe.

Name Index

Sandel, M.J., 46
Schattschneider, E.E., 70
Schmitt, E., 111, 81n3
Schutz, A., 101
Shane, S., 11, 120n4
Shenon, P., 76
Simmons, J.R., 35
Simon, H., 19
Skok, J.E., 133
Spicer, M., xi, 3, 40, 53, 54n1,3, 131,
    132
Staniševski, D., 121
Stivers, C., xi, 43, 45, 48–51, 51, 134
Stone, D.A., xi, 47, 106
Sundquist, J.L., 71

Taylor, C., 3, 46
Terry, L.D., 40

Thompson, F., 33, 34, 38
Toulmin, S.S., 46
Townley, B., 16, 17
Tullock, G., 54n3

Voegeliln, E., 102

Waldo, D., 132, 3, 4, 17, 135
Wallace, B.A., 103, 104
Walzer, M., 46, 52
Wamsley, G.L., 30, 40, 43, 54n5
Weber, M., x, 3, 83, 87, 88, 135
Weschler, L., 137n1
White, J.D., xi, 132
White, L.D., 36
White, O.F., 131, 132

Yanow, D., xi

Subject Index

Kelo v. City of New London, 32

language, 57, 61, 84, 102
  See also writing
liberal (term), 31
liberalism
  classical, 31–32
  See also neoliberalism
linguistics, 58
Locke, John, 41, 93
loop model, x, 4–5, 7, 9–12, 21, 24, 26, 29, 45, 53, 80, 121–22, 130

Machiavelli, Niccolò, 90, 91, 93
managerialism, 15, 56
  neoliberal, 35, 38, 53, 77
  rational, 13, 39
Marcuse, Herbert, 72
market reforms, 29, 124
mercantilism, 93
metanarratives, 57, 60, 67, 71–72, 78, 97
metaphor(s), 25–27, 59, 101–05, 112, 115, 117, 123
  competing, 25
  the "good father," 91
  network, 6
Miller, Judith, 66

neoliberal philosophy, 32–33
neoliberalism, 29–32, 40, 48, 53, 77, 80, 124, 129
  extremism, 37–39
  and government, 32, 34
  in public administration, 33
  and self-interest, 47
  See also liberalism
New Deal, 31
new public management, 17, 29–30, 78, 124
news media, 76–77
  See also broadcast media
Nietzsche, Friedrich, xi, 22, 60, 118
normalization, 128, 132

ontology, 83, 105
orthodoxy, 3–4, 28, 54n2, 55–56, 71–72, 78, 80, 119

orthodoxy *(continued)*
  alternatives, 27–54, 122–26
  and epiphenomenal symbol manipulation, 77
  and neoliberalism, 33, 38, 47–48, 53
  reform of, 71
  rules orientation, 31
outsourcing, 32, 87, 124, 129

panopticism, 128
paradigm anxiety, 29, 45
participation, 79–80, 125
pastoralism, 128, 132
perception, human, 20
performance measurement, 12–13, 16, 34, 36–37, 77
Philosophy and the Mirror of Nature, 123
photograph, the, 58
phronesis, 48
physics, 102–05
Plato, 10, 22, 41, 69
political science, 4, 69
political technology, 89, 92
polyarchy, 9
population, the, 93–94
positivism, 12-13, 16-22, 24, 25, 82
postindustrial society, 60
PowerTrac system, 12, 14
practice, 113–14
presence, 23–24
principal agent theory, 34, 37
privacy, 48
privatization, 6, 29–30, 34–35, 38–39, 78, 124
production, 59–60
professionalism, 49
pseudocommunity, 62
public choice, 30, 34
public interest, 40, 45, 51, 54n5, 74

rational managerialism. *See* managerialism
rationalism, 31, 129
Reagan administration, 30
Reagan, Ronald, 33

About the Authors

Hugh T. Miller is a member of the faculty of the School of Public Administration at Florida Atlantic University, where he holds the rank of professor and serves as School's director. His books include *Postmodern Public Policy*; *Tampering with Tradition: The Unrealized Authority of Democratic Agency*, with Peter Bogason and Sandra Kensen; *These Things Happen: Stories from the Public Sector*, with Mohamad Alkadry; and *Postmodernism, "Reality" and Public Administration: A Discourse*, with Charles J. Fox. His e-mail address is hmiller@fau.edu.

Charles J. Fox was director of the Center for Public Service, and professor of political science at Texas Tech University until his death in May 2004. He received his B.A. from the University of California, Santa Barbara, in intellectual history. His Ph.D. in government was from the Claremont Graduate School. Professor Fox's work has appeared in *American Behavioral Scientist*, *Public Administration Review*, *Public Policy Review*, *Administration & Society*, *American Review of Public Administration*, *Public Personnel Review*, *International Journal of Public Administration*, and *Administrative Theory & Praxis*. Trained in political philosophy, his intellectual project was to bring philosophical scholarship to bear on the problematics of American governance.